Praise f   lren

School choic   lents who are
otherwise lef   give choice a
chance to wo

e 1982–1989
Institution on
ord University

The authors   , innovation,
and the sens   le for school
choice. As th   eart."

llen, President
shington, DC

School choic   tional reform
in America   htful primer
on school ch   policymakers
and activists

ation Director
Institute for Justice, Washington, DC

Bonsteel and Bonilla bring common sense and moral outrage to the crushing problem of public school failure and urge upon us a simple, honorable, and straightforward remedy: school choice. Every other democracy does; in particular, American failure to offer school choice to the poor works a special hardship on those who are most vulnerable. That the First Child attends private school is a metaphor that should not be lost on us.

— *Denis P. Doyle*
Doyle Associates, Chevy Chase, Maryland
Coauthor of Winning the Brain Race

California has long been a hotbed of activity for parental freedom via school choice. . . . Alan Bonsteel and Carlos Bonilla, with *A Choice for Our Children*, have provided great incentive for Californians to unite and finally dislodge the monopolistic status quo. This good book can contribute powerfully to that great cause.

— *Quentin L. Quade, Director*
The Blum Center for Parental Freedom in Education
Marquette University, Milwaukee, Wisconsin

. . . a concise, comprehensive, and cogent treatise of the history and efforts to institute parental choice as a means of restoring both quality and diversity to publicly funded educational opportunities available to the parents and children of California.

— *H. Glenn Davis, Ph.D.*
Former Associate State Superintendent of
Public Instruction for California
Santa Barbara, California

[Bonsteel and Bonilla] graphically illustrate that the problems facing our school system are a result of a diffusion of responsibility for their well-being amongst endless layers of bureaucracy and a loss of accountability of administrators and teachers. . . . *[A Choice for Our Children]* makes an extremely effective case for free school choice. . . . The time for breaking away from the ossified educational policies of the past is *now.*

— *John Tunney, former U.S. Senator*
Santa Monica, California

Vouchers are the only way to achieve real reform in public education. With Dr. Bonsteel's and Dr. Bonilla's many examples of schools and teaching methods that work, it is incredible that public schools are still adopting absurd experiments like Ebonics and Mathland.

— *Deborah Wright*
Candidate for Congress, 1994 and 1996
Administrator, Children's Educational Opportunity Foundation, Oakland
Founder, Stop Ebonics—Educate Our Kids, Oakland

In *A Choice for Our Children*, Alan Bonsteel and Carlos Bonilla clearly describe the heart of the school choice movement; that the fight for school choice is actually the fight for the values that Americans hold dear—liberty and freedom. *A Choice for Our Children* is a must read for parents who feel trapped by America's system of public education. . . .

— *Gordon St. Angelo*
President and CEO
The Milton and Rose D. Friedman Foundation, Indianapolis, Indiana

A Choice for Our Children not only chronicles the superior academic results of schools of choice, but also the untold story of the unique sense of community one finds in schools freely chosen by the families they serve.

— *Cliff Cobb*
Senior Fellow, Redefining Progress, San Francisco
Author of Responsive Schools, Renewed Communities

Other Books by the Authors

Carlos A. Bonilla

Parental Choice in Education: The Good, the Bad, & the Ugly (1992)

School Dropouts: The Tragedy of America's Undereducated Youth (with Jana L. Brazda, 1993)

Perspectives in Multicultural Education: Teaching in the Diverse Classroom (1996)

Hispanic Dropouts: Causes, Frequency, & Solutions (1997)

Public (K-12) Education's Hot Jalapeños: Topics Picantes in Special Education (with Joyce L. Goss, 1997)

Students-at-Risk: The Teachers' Call to Action (with Joyce L. Goss, 1997)

John E. Coons and Stephen D. Sugarman

Private Wealth and Public Education (with William Clune, 1970)

Education by Choice: The Case for Family Control (1978)

Scholarships for Children (1992)

Milton Friedman

Capitalism and Freedom (1962, 1982)

Free to Choose (with Rose D. Friedman, 1980)

Tyranny of the Status Quo (with Rose D. Friedman, 1984)

And about two dozen others.

A Choice
for Our
Children

Curing the Crisis
in America's Schools

Alan Bonsteel and Carlos A. Bonilla

With an exchange of views between
John E. Coons and Milton Friedman

And with contributions by
James Horsman and Stephen D. Sugarman

Institute for Contemporary Studies
San Francisco

Inquiries, book orders, and catalog requests should be addressed to ICS Press, 720
Market Street, 4th Floor, San Francisco, CA 94102. Tel. (415) 981-5353; Fax (415)
986-4878; Internet www.icspress.com. For book orders and catalog requests, call toll
free in the United States: (800) 326-0263.

Cover and interior design by Van Cleve Britton Publishing, Ltd. Book set in Adobe
Garamond and ITC Eras.

0 9 8 7 6 5 4 3 2 1

Library of Congress Cataloging-in-Publication Data
    Bonsteel, Alan, 1951–
        A choice for our children: curing the crisis in America's schools / Alan Bonsteel
    and Carlos A. Bonilla; with an exchange of views between John E. Coons and
    Milton Friedman; and with contributions by James Horsman and Stephen D.
    Sugarman.
            p. cm.
        Includes bibliographical references and index.
        ISBN 1-55815-496-5 (pb)
        1. School choice—United States. 2. School choice—California—Case
    studies. 3. Charter schools—United States. 4. Charter schools—California—
    Case studies. 5. Educational vouchers—United States. 6. Educational vouch-
    ers—California—Case studies. I. Bonilla, Carlos A. II. Title.
    LB1027.9.B65 1997
    379.1'11'0973—dc21
                                                                    97-5230
                                                                        CIP

For up-to-date information on the school choice movement, visit the Web site
www.GetRealEd.org.

Contents

Foreword

Our increasingly competitive world economy requires that we have first-class schools. Growing evidence indicates that choice in education has a powerful effect in improving the quality of our schools—a change which can only benefit all Americans.

Yet the choice in education movement is about far more than just efficiency; its potential reaches well beyond the notion of increasing output from the same inputs. School choice is about how we Americans want to govern our lives in the 21st century.

For the last hundred years, we have been building a state-driven school system. We have consolidated our schools, believing that bigger was better. Is it any wonder that, in an Information Age that requires diversity, flexibility, and speed, our lumbering government schools are not working?

Choice in education offers us the opportunity to return schools to those who make them productive: teachers, principals, parents, and children. Those directly involved—the people who are personally invested in and directly accountable for the fruits of their labor—must have the authority to design schools that work. We must renew the bonds between school and community. This is the only way that we can reenergize our educational system.

Perhaps even more importantly, choice provides the chance to create self-governing enterprises out of our schools. Not only will our children acquire the knowledge and skills to prepare them for a successful future, but they will also learn first-hand what it means for men and women to govern their own lives and the institutions that affect them.

Books such as *A Choice for Our Children* are an essential part of the fight to rescue our failing school system. ICS is proud to bring to the American public this critical information about how choice in education can stimulate *real* change, ensuring hope and prosperity for our children.

Robert B. Hawkins, Jr., President
Institute for Contemporary Studies

Introduction

A revolution in education is taking place in the United States as we near the twenty-first century. In more than thirty states, efforts are under way to empower families with the right to choose the best possible schools for their children within a system of open competition and freedom of choice.

Education is the basis for all that we do, for all that we hold dear. It transcends all other issues in importance. No challenge facing our society—preserving world peace, combating poverty, overcoming racial tensions, protecting the environment—can be met successfully if we fail to pass on our knowledge and values to the next generation. And yet, tragically, the evidence is overwhelming that our system of compulsory public elementary and secondary education has failed.

American schoolchildren consistently rank at or near the bottom in international comparisons of educational achievement, despite per student spending greater than that of any other country in the world. Equally shocking is that our public schools have become truly dangerous places: the safety of our children can no longer be assured. And, in an Information Age in which adaptation and change are essential, our public schools themselves remain rigidly bureaucratic anachronisms.

One obvious reason for the failure of our public schools is that the United States remains the only major industrialized nation in the world in which school choice at the elementary and secondary levels is virtually nonexistent. When Sweden began to change over to a voucher system in 1992, the United States was left isolated and alone as the most monopolistic and bureaucratic nation with regards to schooling.

By contrast, at the higher education level in the United States, the battle for school choice has long since been won. Beginning with the GI Bill of

Rights in 1944 and continuing with Pell Grants and government-guaranteed student loans that make private as well as public universities accessible to all, the American people have established a system of higher education based on freedom of choice that is the world's envy. American universities attract students from every continent.

In the battle for school choice in the United States, California is the grand prize. Not only is it by far the most populous state, but it is often the leader in national trends. With a population exceptionally open to innovation, and a technology-based economy that demands highly educated workers who can be competitive in cutting-edge industries, California can no longer tolerate the failure of its public schools. Already, polls show that in principle, three out of four Californians support the concept of school choice.

California is also fortunate enough to have a well-trained, dedicated base of school choice activists who have been working in the field since the first serious effort in 1978, and a well-financed organization, the School Futures Research Foundation, led by individuals of uncommon vision and altruism. It is possible, of course, that educational choice's Holy Grail—the establishment of a statewide system of choice that will demonstrate the value of the concept and serve as a model for other states—may be achieved in another state first. But when Californians vote for school choice, the war will be all but won.

This book tells the story of the battle for educational choice in the United States, with a special emphasis on California. Part I focuses on the evidence for school choice and a brief history of some of the early efforts in the field. Part II profiles seven of California's independent schools and allows us to share our passion for the academic excellence, innovation, and sense of community that result from school choice. Part III describes current efforts for school choice in California and in other states, ongoing controversies in the field, and our prospects for success.

Half of the chapters are collaborative efforts by Alan Bonsteel and Carlos A. Bonilla. The other half were written exclusively by one of us, or by one or more of our four guest contributors, to whom we are grateful for adding so much of value to the book.

The school choice story is an inspiring one. Years ago, Gandhi said, "When your cause is just, people will come from out of nowhere to help you." Both of us have witnessed, again and again, public-spirited citizens coming from "out of nowhere" and setting aside all thought of personal gain to help with this most vital of causes.

The great educator Maria Montessori often spoke of the bond uniting those who work in the service of children. For both of us, this inspiring work has led to deep and lasting friendships with many others in the field. As in any endeavor about which the participants feel passionately, there have been disagreements along the way, some of which are chronicled in this book. Despite our differences, however, we feel a profound respect for all of our colleagues and friends who have worked in the field. We hope we haven't forgotten to mention some of those key people in California who have worked long and hard to make the dream of school choice a reality.

Alan Bonsteel, M.D.
San Francisco, California

Carlos A. Bonilla, Ph.D., M.D.
Stockton, California

March 1997

Part I

It is not the critic who counts, not the man who points out how the strong man stumbled or where the doer of deeds could have done them better. The credit goes to the man who is actually in the arena, whose face is marred by dust and sweat and blood; who strives valiantly; who errs and comes short again and again; who knows the great enthusiasms, the great devotions, and spends himself in a worthy cause; who, at the best, knows the triumph of high achievement; and who, at the worst, if he fails, at least fails while daring greatly, so that his place shall never be with those cold and timid souls who know neither victory nor defeat.

— THEODORE ROOSEVELT

Chapter 1

The Lost Generation

Alan Bonsteel

I saw the fear in the teenager's eyes as he stumbled through the back door of my emergency room, blood splattered across his shirt, his arm hooked around his buddy's neck for support. "Don't let me die!" he pleaded.

He had taken a bullet in his right chest—the safer side if you have to take a hit, but there's never any way to know a slug's pathway. We boosted him onto the gurney, and I called the orders the nurses knew without being told: oxygen by mask, two big-bore IVs, lactated Ringer's solution wide open, type and cross six units, call for type O Negative in case we needed it in a hurry. With no time for anything more than local anesthesia, I punched in a chest tube to suction the blood and keep the lung expanded—a bloody mess.

A chest x-ray showed the bullet had lodged far from the heart and great vessels. He would live. Tragically, too many have died.

From my vantage point as a family physician doing my share of emergency room shifts, our failure to prepare our youth for a productive, responsible life isn't just an abstraction; it's something that hits me over the head every day, usually within hours or even minutes after starting my shift. And this wasn't an inner-city ER, either; this was Atwater, population 21,000, a formerly sleepy California farm town now plagued by gangs and drugs.

The kids I see are basically good kids. They want to do well; they want a sense of meaning and purpose in life. Unfortunately, many don't stand much of a chance. It's not just the failure of our schools to teach them basic educa-

tional survival skills; it's also our failure to pass on the values of our civiliza-
tion. One is tempted to say that teaching morals and ethics belongs in the
home, but for most kids who come from dysfunctional or even abusive families, the best chance for stability and values training is in school.

And if they don't stay in school, we've lost them altogether. Our high
school dropout rates remain shockingly high. Still, the stories these kids tell
me about the lethal weaponry floating around the schools, of school officials
who aspire to little more than survival in a dysfunctional system, and of the
alienation the kids feel, make me wonder sometimes how *any* of them tough it
out to graduation day.

In 1994, the national Council of the Great City Schools reported that 83
percent of big-city school superintendents and school board members listed
violence and gang activities as their number one concern. Stories about weapons in schools—even those in many "nice" suburbs—have become so common
as to lose their shock value.

The *Los Angeles Times* has characterized the Los Angeles Unified School
District (LAUSD) as "a school system where violence, gang rivalries, and drug
problems tend to be everyday realities." A study conducted jointly in March
1997 by the American Civil Liberties Union, the California State University
at Los Angeles, and the University of Southern California revealed that 14
percent of the students at eleven representative high schools in Los Angeles
brought weapons to school, including 2.5 percent who had brought a gun at
least once. The report stated that the LAUSD's implementation of a policy for
using metal detectors to keep weapons out of the schools had "clearly been
unsuccessful." Two-thirds of the students surveyed said the devices had no
impact on the number of weapons in their school. One respondent, from
Jordan High School in the heart of South Central Los Angeles, wrote on the
survey form, "The students here know nothing but how to be violent."

During the last twenty years, American public school spending per student has increased *more than 80 percent* in constant (inflation-adjusted) dollars;
in California it has increased 40 percent. But instead of improvements, we
find academic quality so poor in public schools that *public school teachers* are
enrolling their own children in private schools at much higher rates than the

general public. Our American public schools are operating at a *60 percent failure rate,* with at least 20 percent of students dropping out and half of those who do finish graduating with a seventh-grade education or less. Many graduates cannot even read the diplomas they are given. In California, more than half of the freshmen entering the California State University system must take remedial mathematics and English courses.

According to United States Department of Education statistics, we stand *dead last* among the world's Western democracies in school performance, and behind even some developing countries such as Korea. The much-publicized Third International Mathematics and Science Study in November 1996 ranked American schoolchildren far below their overseas peers. The authoritative statistics of the International Organization for Economic Cooperation and Development painted an even gloomier picture, placing American public school students at the *bottom* in the skills we should be best at: science and math.

In 1983, the now famous *A Nation at Risk* report shocked America by warning of "A Rising Tide of Mediocrity," and jarred us by saying,

> *If an unfriendly power had attempted to impose on America the mediocre educational performance that exists today, we might well have viewed it as an act of war.*

Although public school quality is a problem everywhere in the United States, it is in a state of crisis in our inner cities, where in some schools dropout rates exceed 60 percent and *none* of those being given diplomas are graduating at grade level. Perhaps it is not surprising, then, that it was in the inner city of Milwaukee—a city notorious for its abandon-all-hope public schools—that America saw one of its first experiments in a system of open competition and freedom of choice in education, modeled after the highly successful GI Bill of Rights. This breakthrough for our children was achieved by a remarkable woman named Polly Williams.

Chapter 2

The Polly Williams Story

It is October 6, 1991. On a *60 Minutes* TV documentary, Mike Wallace is describing the dramatic success of a K–12 school choice program—one of the nation's very few programs that include private schools.

"Urban Day School is the largest of six private elementary schools that are taking part in Milwaukee's Choice plan," Wallace says. "Urban Day kids wear uniforms. They walk single-file in the halls. They clean up after themselves. And in the classroom, they get individual attention and a curriculum that emphasizes African-American culture and history. And who is behind the Milwaukee Choice Plan? Polly Williams, a Wisconsin state legislator. But before she was a legislator, she was a welfare mother of four."

The camera pans to Polly Williams, who says, "This parental choice program was created for children whose needs were not being addressed in the public schools. . . . They have not done a good job at all. Sixty percent of the kids who enter school do not complete, and of the 40 percent who walk across that stage and get that certificate of attendance, 40 percent of *them* can't even read the certificate. . . . Something is wrong with that system."

Cut to Mike Wallace grilling the president of the local public school teachers union. "You make 80,000 bucks a year as the head of the teachers union. Your own teachers make $30,000 a year. These teachers make half that or less, and they seem to have inspired something here that I would think you would want to come down here and take a good look at," Wallace demands. "Yet all you do is talk about the educational establishment."

"No, no, no, sir, that's not true," the squirming union president protests. "Our organization has been advocating change for years. But we're told over and over again, 'No, that'll cost too much.'"

Cut back to Polly Williams. "Why is it that $6,000 per child is not enough money for you to figure out a program to educate those children?" she demands. "We're doing tremendously well for a third of the cost and with a 98 percent graduation rate."

"And what do you think of Ted Kennedy—white, liberal Democrat," Wallace asks. "Good man? He opposes school choice."

"Hey, not for himself," Williams replies. "All *his* kids went to private schools. So, you know, I kind of question these people whose children are safely in these nice schools talking about what they don't want for poor people."

After moving with her family from Mississippi to Wisconsin as a nine-year-old, Polly Williams attended Milwaukee public schools. Later, as a single mother of four, medical problems briefly forced her onto welfare. By the time her children were old enough for school, Milwaukee's public schools had become dangerous and decrepit. Williams scrimped and saved to put her four children through the private Urban Day School, the very school that is now the most active participant in her choice program.

Urban Day, however, stopped at the eighth grade, and there were no affordable private high schools. Reluctantly, she sent her oldest daughter to public school. When her daughter was assigned to be bussed to a high school Williams considered inferior, Williams petitioned the Milwaukee public school district for a transfer. She was turned down. She then barged into the superintendent's office. Finding it empty, she left a note: "My name is Polly Williams. I live at 1437 Burleigh Street. I will not send my child to the school you've assigned. You may come and arrest me."

"Then," Williams recalls, holding her wrists together as if for handcuffs, "I went home to wait." The superintendent relented. Williams got the school she wanted.

Now a seven-term Democratic state representative from Milwaukee's Near North Side, and Jesse Jackson's Wisconsin campaign chairman in 1984 and 1988, Williams led her constituents to an amazing victory in 1990: a pilot voucher program for 1,000 low-income children from Milwaukee. From the start, her arguments were inspired by the civil rights struggle of Dr. Martin Luther King, Jr.

"The way I see it," Williams says, "the system is preparing our children for slavery. Drop out by the tenth grade, get into the street life. When you should be walking across the stage getting a diploma, you're standing in front of a judge wearing chains. Parental choice is the difference between empowerment and enslavement. We gotta fight. I'll be the one leading the revolt to destroy the system."

Her troops were mostly mothers on Aid to Families with Dependent Children, many of them without a dollar to spare. She realized that their strength was in their simple, strong desire for a better life for their children, and she pressed for a public hearing. "My idea was," Williams recalls, "if you want to tell us no, then you're going to have to tell us to our face."

Polly Williams, the former welfare mom who dared the public school authorities to have her arrested for refusing to send her child to an inferior school. She eventually became a Wisconsin state legislator and started the now-famous Milwaukee school voucher program, becoming a heroine to all in the educational freedom movement. (Photo courtesy of Annette Polly Williams.)

Typical of her supporters was Mikel Holt, a former public school parent and a leading voice for education reform in Milwaukee's black community. "In the public schools, parents don't have rights," he says. "The teachers union dictates policy. You often have incompetent teachers in the classrooms. My question is simple: Why would I give my son's life over to them?"

At the hearing in February 1990, two hundred parents and children came to demand school choice, cheering and stomping as Williams shouted, "We want self-determination, not handouts and dependency." The bill for her low-income voucher program passed the Wisconsin Legislature on a 49–48 vote and was signed into law by Governor Tommy Thompson in April 1990. Following the little-known Vermont program for private school vouchers in rural areas, in existence since 1869 (see Chapter 31), the Milwaukee program was only the second elementary- and secondary-level school choice program in the United States to include private schools.

The public education establishment immediately sued. But with the help of attorney Clint Bolick, then of the Landmark Legal Foundation and now of the Institute for Justice, Polly Williams prevailed. The Wisconsin Supreme Court declined an injunction against the new educational choice program by a 4–3 vote, and the children were able to start school that fall. Five months later, the *New York Times* reported,

> As the program's first semester draws to a close, the parents speak in jubilant tones about their children's progress, directors of the six participating private schools describe a relatively smooth transition, and seven-year-old Javon Williams, for one, says that for the first time he looks forward to school.

A few weeks later, Polly Williams received a letter from Governor Bill Clinton of Arkansas, praising her "innovative and visionary program," an opinion he later reconsidered, after accepting large political contributions from the National Education Association for his presidential campaign.

Among the many hurdles thrown in front of the Milwaukee program was a stacked deck from the outset in its evaluation. The "researcher" for this task was designated by the state superintendent of instruction, Herbert Grover, a vocal opponent of any competition for his public schools. To no one's surprise, he chose someone who also made no secret of his opposition to educational choice, a man named John Witte.

In arrogant disregard for the taxpayers paying for the study, until recently the only person with total access to the raw data gathered on the Milwaukee program was Witte himself. Thus, while some of the data could be gleaned from his reports, a good deal of it has been released selectively so as to deliberately bias the evaluation.

Some outcomes of the Milwaukee program have always been beyond dispute. There is absolutely no question that the program has resulted in increased family satisfaction: in every year studied, the participants have reported by at least a 97 percent margin that they are happier than with their previous public school. No one seriously claims that the Milwaukee program has resulted in more racial segregation; by any rational standard, the private schools participating in the program are *better* integrated than Milwaukee's public schools. And everyone agrees that the participating private schools are much safer and have done a much better job of controlling school-site violence.

Of the two charges by Witte that are in hot dispute, the first is the claim that the school choice program has not improved achievement scores. Witte arrived at this erroneous conclusion by pitting children in the Milwaukee program, all of whom came from low-income and generally low-education families, against *all* of Milwaukee's public school children, including those from the highest-income, best-educated families. When these factors were properly controlled by impartial researchers, the kids in the Milwaukee program *have* shown improved test scores compared with their cohorts in the public schools.

Second, Witte characterized attrition from the program as "high," a remark that was picked up by much of the national news media. In fact, attrition in the program has been *lower* than for children from the same socioeconomic groups in Milwaukee's public schools.[1]

---

[1] For more in-depth information about these issues, see *Break These Chains* by Daniel McGroarty (San Francisco: ICS Press, 1996).

Fortunately, the dispute may have been laid to rest with the recent publication of two important independent studies. The first, a joint study by researchers from Harvard University and the University of Houston that was released in August 1996, compared 1,034 students in the Milwaukee program with 407 students who had applied but had been turned down for lack of space—in other words, children from the same socioeconomic group who had gone to public school rather than a private school in the Milwaukee program. The study found that, by the fourth year of the program, the voucher students scored eleven percentage points higher on standardized tests in math and nearly five percentage points higher in reading—in schools that were costing the taxpayers *half* of the per student public school spending.

The second study, by Cecilia Elena Rouse, an assistant professor of economics and public policy at Princeton University, was released in January 1997. Her research demonstrated that participants in the Milwaukee program gained 1.5 to 2.0 percentage points *per year* in their math scores when compared with their peers from equivalent socioeconomic groups—once again, in a program that costs half as much per student as the public schools.

The Milwaukee school choice program has been so successful and so overwhelmingly popular that, for the beginning of the 1996–97 school year, the Wisconsin Legislature voted to increase its size tenfold, from approximately 1,500 children to 15,000, and to include religious schools for the first time, thereby greatly expanding the options available to families.

Once again, the public school establishment immediately sued. In January 1997, a low-level district judge known from the outset to have teachers-union ties struck down both the inclusion of religious schools, on the grounds that it conflicted with the Wisconsin Constitution, and the expansion of the program, on the grounds that a procedural error had been made in the way the legislation was authorized—a point of view not shared by the Wisconsin Legislature.

As of early 1997, the Milwaukee program is continuing with the original limit of 1,500 children. The procedural problems can be rectified simply by having the Wisconsin Legislature reauthorize the program's expansion. On January 21, 1997, Polly Williams and Wisconsin state senator Robert Welch announced that they would reintroduce a bill to expand the program to 15,000 participants, this time disallowing religious schools from participating until a favorable ruling can be obtained from the Wisconsin Supreme Court or the United States Supreme Court, whichever comes first.

The attempt by the public school system to strangle in the cradle a program that has undeniably benefited thousands of disadvantaged children— not because of any meaningful dispute about the results but precisely because it made the public schools look bad, threatening their monopoly—will thwart the efforts of many poor families to work toward a better life for their children. What is doubly ironic, in addition to the obvious jealousy of the public school establishment over the success of the Milwaukee program, is that Milwaukee's public schools are *so* bad that the public school teachers themselves are putting their own children into private schools at a rate almost 40 percent higher than that of the general public.

In the long run, however, the public school monopoly's legal harassment of this program, and of the similar program started in Cleveland in 1996, may be a classic example of shooting oneself in the foot. There is no question that either the Milwaukee program or the Cleveland program will soon be tested for constitutionality in the United States Supreme Court; and there is little doubt that, with the Court's current makeup, either one will easily pass constitutional muster. As tragic as it is that thousands of deserving Milwaukee children are currently being denied a better education, in the long run it may be for the best that the ultimate battle will take place on ground that is favorable to school choice advocates. It is in the interest of *all* of the nation's children to see a quick victory for the constitutionality of school choice in the highest court in the land.

Chapter 3

A School for the Next Century

A few short years ago, the Vaughn Street Elementary School in Pacoima in the San Fernando Valley of California had all the problems typical of an inner-city public school: depressingly low test scores, a deteriorating physical plant, a more than 50 percent turnover in teachers every two years, and very little parental participation. In 1993, however, a dramatic turnaround began. Under dynamic new leadership, priorities were reordered, teachers took a greater degree of ownership of the school, and families became involved. Best of all, test scores have risen significantly every year for the past three years, increasing from the tenth percentile to greater than the fortieth percentile.

What changed? The Vaughn Street School—now renamed the Vaughn Next Century Learning Center—was one of the first in California to take advantage of the opportunity to become a *charter school* under a state law passed in 1992. Under the direction of principal Yvonne Chan, the school was placed under community control as a locally governed charter school. With the freedom to set the school's priorities in consultation with the teachers and parents, Chan cut expenses by putting services such as payroll and stocking the cafeteria out to competitive bid. With the money saved, she built a new wing of fourteen computer-equipped classrooms and added new teachers, lowering the student/teacher ratio from 33-to-1 to 27-to-1.

This year a further reduction to 20-to-1 has occurred in grades one through three, as a result of Governor Pete Wilson's class-size-reduction program. Teachers are now expected to work longer hours, but they have more authority and higher salaries. The school year has been lengthened from 180 days to 200 days. An after-school soccer program instills character and sportsmanship and keeps the children involved, and a Saturday Museum of Art program introduces them to the cultural life of the region. A health program coordinates various community services for medical, dental, and vision examinations. By January of 1997, the school had managed to cut its overhead sufficiently to achieve another stunning success: it broke ground again—this time for a $2.2 million facility that will house a community library, ten new classrooms, science labs, and a teacher training center.

The excitement of the transformation the school has undergone is obvious from the moment a visitor approaches it. The colorful entryway proudly proclaims GATEWAY TO LEARNING, and freshly painted signs on the school grounds remind students that I AM A WINNER. Of the school's 1,129 students enrolled in the fall of 1996, 972 are Hispanic, almost all of them recent immigrants who spoke no English upon arrival at the school. Yet their families are so pleased to be involved and to be consulted on the changes taking place that they are willing to volunteer at least thirty hours per year helping in the classrooms, and the school boasts a 99.5 percent attendance rate.

The charter school concept is simple. Unlike traditional public schools, to which students are assigned based on geographic residence and which are governed by a bewildering maze of federal, state, county, and local mandates—and by education codes as lengthy as California's eleven volumes (about 100,000 Sections!)—charter schools are public schools financed with a percentage of their state educational funding, run by the local community, and, most importantly, *freely chosen by the families.* No one can be forced into a charter school, and no one can be stopped from leaving if they are dissatisfied.

The concept is generally credited in the United States to educator Ray Budde.[1] It has been endorsed by no less than President Clinton and by the late Albert Shanker, president of the American Federation of Teachers. While the first American charter school was not established until 1991, in Minnesota, Great Britain has had operational charter schools under the name "grant-main-

---

[1] Ray Budde, *Education by Charter: Restructuring School Districts* (Andover, MA: Regional Laboratory for Educational Improvement of the Northeast and Islands, 1988).

tained schools" since 1988, with documented success. As of early 1997, twenty-one states have charter school laws—although not all of these states actually have charter schools yet. This exciting new development in American education was chronicled in a *Time* magazine cover story entitled "New Hope for Public Schools" on October 31, 1994. According to Jeanne Allen's Center for Education Reform in Washington, DC, the United States had 80,000 students in 412 charter schools in 13 states, as of the fall of 1996.

In California, although legislation to establish charter schools was introduced as early as 1990, it was effectively blocked by the California Teachers Association until 1992, when the school voucher initiative that ultimately became known as Proposition 174 qualified for the ballot. This provided the motivation for California's educational establishment to be seen as also supporting school choice, and they grudgingly acquiesced to allowing a pilot program of 100 charter schools. The bill, authored by state senator Gary Hart, passed in 1992 and became effective January 1, 1993. Since that time, the Pacific Research Institute's Center for Innovation in Education has been especially effective in promoting charter schools in California. It has won three important legal cases on behalf of charter schools assaulted via the courts by a public school establishment jealous of their success and threatened by the new competition.

In a state with roughly 10,000 public schools, the limit of 100 charter schools, most of which are much smaller than traditional public schools, has restricted public school choice to only about $^1/_2$ percent of California's public school students. The charter schools are funded at much lower per student levels than traditional public schools, receiving only the state Average Daily Attendance money, but *not* their share of local school tax money, and very little in federal aid to education. They are also required to spend about *one-fifth* of their ADA funding on administration by their sponsoring district, even though, as community-governed schools, the benefit to the charter schools of this district-level administration is highly questionable.[2]

California reached its limit of 100 charter schools in early 1996. In March of that year, the state's watchdog Little Hoover Commission issued a report

---

[2] For additional perspective on this mandatory administrative spending by charter schools, see the sidebar "The 95/5 Hoax," in Chapter 33.

investigating the performance of charter schools to date.[3] A brief summary of its findings:

> The performance of schools in California and across the nation is widely recognized as falling short. Students compare poorly with their counterparts in other nations; businesses complain that recent graduates cannot do entry-level jobs and lack a good work ethic. . . .

> The Commission visited twenty-six charter schools, more than one-fourth of the operational schools in California. . . . The Commission saw evidence of the explosion of energy and the strong community links that occur when teachers, parents, and others are given the opportunity to implement their own programs and procedures.

> Charter schools can be judged at least a partial success on the basis of a variety of criteria. These include:

> ➤ **Parental Satisfaction.** The student population in charter schools is there by choice. Almost all charter schools have waiting lists for admission, and most have a high rate of retention year to year.
> ➤ **Economic Value.** Many charter schools have found ways to trim costs in order to redirect resources into the classroom.
> ➤ **Academic Innovation**. Not only are charter schools different from their district counterparts, but very few resemble each other. Academic approaches range from Montessori and Waldorf to humanistic and open.
> ➤ **Enhanced Opportunities for Teachers.** In many charter schools, teachers drive policy, shaping curriculum, networking for continuity, and controlling working conditions.
> ➤ **Increased Focus on Low-Achieving Students.** Large urban charter schools and many independent-study charter schools focus on low-achieving students, bringing them programs designed to meet their needs.
> ➤ **Avoidance of Discrimination.** Charter schools have demonstrated an ethnic balance that reflects that found in statewide schools. Some

---

[3] "The Charter Movement: Education Reform, School by School," March 1996. Available from the Little Hoover Commission, 660 J St., Suite 260, Sacramento, CA 95814. Telephone (916) 445-2125.

of the largest cater to students who are socioeconomically disadvantaged.

The Little Hoover Commission's report concluded that, "School by school, the educational system is being asked to shift from accountability for following rules to accountability for results." It recommended lifting the artificial limit of 100 on the number of charter schools permitted, and it recommended allowing them even more autonomy to be responsive to the communities they serve.

Charter schools have proved themselves beyond any reasonable doubt. One of the next battles in the school choice movement in California will surely be to expand the number of allowable charter schools—preferably by removing the limit altogether—and to protect them from bureaucratic interference. Slow progress is already being made, in the form of individual waivers being granted by the state Board of Education for charter school applications submitted by local school districts. As of March 1997, there are 120 charters in existence—for schools all across California, from rural areas to the inner cities—and several new ones are being granted each month.

The basic idea of choice in government-funded programs is hardly new, of course, so it came as no surprise that charter schools work, and work well. Our Medicare and Medicaid programs allow free choice of health care providers; the food stamp program allows a free choice of supermarkets and food; we have freedom of education at the preschool level (supported by a national preschool voucher program; see Chapter 14); and we have had freedom of choice in higher education since the days when our servicemen and women sailed home in troop ships from victory in World War II, taking part in a program that is as American as Mom and apple pie: the GI Bill of Rights.

Chapter 4

The GI Bill—Granddaddy of Them All

Alan Bonsteel

My father went to college on the GI Bill of Rights, and his two younger brothers followed in his footsteps. They had defeated Hitler and saved the world for democracy. Anything was possible, and a grateful nation bestowed upon its servicemen and women an unprecedented opportunity: a college education or trade school at the taxpayers' expense, with the *freedom to choose* for oneself.

My father's graduation photo sat on our mantle all through my childhood. The first college graduate in our family, he was surrounded in the photo by glowing family and friends as he proudly wore his mortarboard and gown and waved his hard-won diploma. I remember, when I sat next to him as he helped me with my homework, that if I got stuck he would urge me to "give it the old college try," and I would sense in him the pride, the determination, and the hard work that had gone into his college degree.

Confident of victory, President Franklin D. Roosevelt signed the GI Bill into law on June 22, 1944, only two weeks after D-Day. Formally known as the Servicemen's Readjustment Act, the bill provided not only for educational benefits for returning servicemen and women, but also for medical care, housing assistance, and job benefits. What rewrote the American dream, however, was the opportunity for a college education—like my father, many GIs were the first in their families to attain this goal.

America's colleges had never seen such students. A *Fortune* magazine study of the class of 1947 showed that veterans made up 70 percent of the class and that the graduates were "the most mature, most responsible, and most self-disciplined group" of college students in history. The University of California's president, Robert Sproul, dubbed them "D.A.R.s"—Damned Average Raisers. At the University of Minnesota, only three of 6,000 ex-GIs were in academic trouble. When one young history professor at Princeton found that his grades failed to follow anything like a normal curve, he sought the advice of the oldest professor in the department. The answer was short and to the point: "Of course they won't follow a normal curve. You're teaching GIs."

Marjorie Raish, an English instructor at the University of Kansas in Lawrence, said in an interview with the *Kansas City Star* in 1946, "They have that priceless quality which is the answer to every teacher's prayer: they want to learn. . . . I wish I could be sure that a single student learned as much as I. I have stowed away on innumerable transports and bombers; I have sat in on so many briefing sessions that I could conduct one myself; I know exactly what to do if I am ever left afloat on a raft. What I learned increased my respect for the GIs daily. They write unashamedly of their religion, and I find it not to be a spineless emotion but a vital force."

Having lived through both the Great Depression and a World War, the GIs were anxious to catch up. When a reporter stopped ex-serviceman Donald Duggleby at Indiana University, he barely paused to say, "Pardon me, but you'll have to hurry. Problems? The main problem of everybody is to catch up. We're all trying to get where we would have been if there hadn't been a war." Many completed their courses of study in a fraction of the usual time. When an English class at Tufts College in Boston came to the lines by poet Andrew Marvell, *But at my back I always hear/ Time's winged chariot hurrying near,* one returning serviceman exclaimed, "Why, that Joe really speaks our language— that's just how I've felt for years."

Many ex-GIs, eager to get on with their lives, started families while still in school—the beginning of the Baby Boom that is now pushing middle age. Family villages sprouted on campus, and parents cooperated by tending daycare centers in shifts. At Southern Methodist University, when ex-GI Buddy King marched across the stage in June of 1947 to claim his hard-won diploma, his son brought down the house with the excited cry, "That's my daddy!"

Between the tidal wave of new students hitting the schools and the large number of families with babies, housing was jam-packed. Student families set up households in attics, cellars, and house trailers. At Rhode Island State, eleven students were crammed into each Quonset hut. The president of Ohio's Marietta College took in boarders. Some hardy students at UCLA slept in parked cars and at all-night movies.

In the decade from 1939 to 1949, enrollment in all U.S. colleges and universities increased by *80 percent,* reaching a peak enrollment of 2,457,000 in the fall of 1949. Virtually all of that growth occurred immediately after the war (data for the wartime years are unavailable, but enrollment must have dropped sharply before picking up again in the fall of 1945), meaning that our college capacity *nearly doubled in four years.* In Plattsburgh, New York, in an amazing demonstration of Yankee can-do spirit, a military base was converted into Champlain College in only three months.

Of the 15 million returning GIs eligible for educational benefits, more than 7 million, or almost half, attended a college or trade school under the GI Bill—including 250,000 blacks, almost all of whom were the first college-goers in their families. At a cost of $5.5 billion, the original GI Bill produced 450,000 engineers, 240,000 accountants, 238,000 teachers, 67,000 doctors, 22,000 dentists, and countless thousands of other professionals—not to mention the legions of clergymen who attended seminaries at taxpayer expense.

For those who chose not to go to college, trade and vocational schools offered an extraordinary array of opportunities. Returning GIs learned to become machinists or photographers, or were trained to repair the amazing new electronic marvel of the age: the television. Many studied for careers in aviation, with millions of Americans taking to travel through the skies following the technological advances of the Second World War.

A study by the Joint Economic Committee of Congress showed that by 1987, those who had attended college under the GI Bill of Rights earned an average of $19,000 more per year than veterans who did not attend. The committee's economist estimated that for each dollar spent on a veteran's education, the nation's output of goods and services increased between $5.00 and $12.50 in constant dollars.

The original GI Bill was followed by Korean and Vietnam War-era veterans bills. These were the inspiration for Federal Pell Grants (and their California equivalents, Cal-Grants) for low-income students attending universities and for government-guaranteed student loans that help deserving young people attend a college of their choice. By the GI Bill's fiftieth anniversary in 1994, some 20.4 million Americans had participated. The freedom of choice and open competition among educational institutions brought about by these programs helped to make America's higher education system the envy of the world, and the GI Bill is now serving as the model for educational choice systems at the elementary and secondary levels throughout the nation.

It is instructive to turn the clock back to 1944 and see how closely the current arguments against freedom of choice at the elementary and secondary levels parallel the objections voiced against the highly successful GI Bill.

In 1944, some said that the GIs would never be able to make good choices for themselves. A few did make poor choices, of course, but most chose carefully and well—and even the questionable decisions often led to valuable opportunities that would not have arisen in a coercive system of education. Many critics pointed out that our colleges and universities were already full. They were, but, as described above, the free market responded to the demand with an explosive growth in capacity to accommodate the returning GIs. Still others claimed that the GI Bill violated the constitutional separation of church and state. In fact, however, colleges such as Notre Dame, Brandeis, Brigham Young, and Calvary Bible College were all treated equally and impartially, and the GI Bill proved so constitutionally sound that it easily withstood every legal challenge.

The GI Bill is a part of American history that lives on today. It was the engine for the postwar economic boom that made the United States the undisputed leader of the free world. It began our transformation from an industrial society to an information-based society. It put education squarely at the center of American life, following an era when few went to college. Although the original college graduates under the GI Bill are now pushing retirement age, their sons and daughters—the Baby Boomers—are now among our nation's leaders. Hardly a citizen today is untouched by this extraordinary chapter in our history, and the vision and inspiration of the framers of the GI Bill live on in American life.

Education is the key to all that we do, to all that we hold dear. With the continuing decline of our public school system, a "GI Bill" for elementary and secondary education is looking better all the time. We could do a lot worse than to, as the returning GIs used to say, give it the old college try.

Chapter 5

America's Berlin Wall

Alan Bonsteel

When I had last been in Berlin, in 1988, the Wall still stood. The train trip through East Germany by night had been eerie, passing by row after row of barbed wire and hurtling past train stations boarded up since the end of World War II. Little did I guess that, within a year, the gates would be thrown open. When that day finally came, I watched on television as delirious crowds danced to Beethoven's "Ode to Joy."

Now, in April of 1993, I was returning to a reborn Berlin. Despite the problems of reunification, there was hope in the air, and an excitement befitting one of the world's most cosmopolitan cities.

I was attending the annual conference of the European Council of National Associations of Independent Schools (ECNAIS). Berlin had been chosen as the site because of the rapidly emerging independent school sector in the former Soviet Union and its satellites. Following the lead of their Western European counterparts, the governments of Russia, Belarus, Latvia, Lithuania, Poland, Hungary, Bulgaria, and the new Czech and Slovak Republics had established initiatives to support new independent schools and break the state school monopolies. Those of us from the more affluent countries subsidized the travel of our colleagues from the former communist bloc, and seventy delegates from fourteen countries, including six former communist countries, gathered in the city that, more than any other, symbolizes the rebirth of freedom in Eastern Europe.

This chapter is adapted from an article that originally appeared in the *National Review,* September 20, 1993. Copyright ©1993 by *National Review,* Inc., 215 Lexington Avenue, New York, NY 10016. Reprinted by permission.

The conference was held at the Kreuzberg Waldorfschule, a school that in many ways symbolizes Germany's free schools. During the Second World War, Hitler outlawed the "nonconformist" Waldorf and Montessori schools. The Nazis also closed all Jewish private schools and cracked down with an iron fist on Germany's Catholic schools. After the war, the West Germans, determined never to repeat this mistake, guaranteed in their new constitution the right of all children, regardless of family income, to a private school education. Although the German government has never appropriated enough money to allow this concept to grow to its full potential, more than 6 percent of all elementary and secondary students in the new unified Germany attend independent schools that get along nicely with about two-thirds of the per student expenditures of the public schools. Now independent schools are proliferating in the former East Germany as well.

The Kreuzberg Waldorf school is in a poor part of the city in an old building that at one time stood in the shadow—literally—of the Berlin Wall. After the wall came down, the school acquired an old Stasi Secret Police station nearby in the former East Berlin. The wires in the building that had been used to bug telephones in the neighborhood were torn out and used as building materials for the playground, and the new annex became known affectionately as the "hole-in-the-wall school." The eighth-graders of the school performed for us Schiller's *Wilhelm Tell*, a play that embodies the spirit of this school: freedom.

In the continuing debate about freedom in schooling in the United States, many commentators still overlook just how far out of step the American centralized system of elementary and secondary government education is with the educational systems of the other Western democracies. *All* of the world's developed countries offer more freedom of choice than we do in the United States. Examples range from England's "Assisted Places" scheme, in which the government awards private school scholarships to 40,000 low-income students, to the true voucher system of the Netherlands, in which fully three-quarters of all of the country's students attend private schools supported by the government at the same per student rate as the public schools.

Having visited independent schools—or voucher schools, if you prefer— in twelve countries, I was at the conference to learn the latest trends in freedom in schooling, and to represent (alone, as it turned out) the United States. Europeans are well aware of the poor quality of American public education and the frightening problems of drugs and violence in our public schools. I wasn't altogether surprised, therefore, when I was asked to be the first speaker and to report on the many state initiatives for educational choice.

At the break, I was approached by one of Poland's delegates, a delightful, bubbly physicist named Elzbieta Putkiewicz. With an ear-to-ear smile, she enthused, "Poland now has 500 free schools supported by the Solidarity government at 30 to 50 percent of the public school rate per student. Maybe you Americans could learn from our experience!"

"That's very interesting," I replied, "but what do you mean 30 to 50 percent? How does the government decide which it will be?"

"Oh, it's not like that," she laughed. "The government just doesn't know how much it's spending!"

I had to laugh as well. In our own campaign for educational choice in California, school district after school district had claimed to be spending *less* than the basic Average Daily Attendance subsidy from the state, without even counting federal, county, and local spending on education. In well over one hundred debates with public school officials, I had never come across even one who could give an accurate and honest accounting of per student spending in his or her district.

Throughout Eastern Europe, the winds of freedom are blowing. Russia has 200 independent schools supported by government tuition scholarships, including new "ecology" schools. Seventy years of communism did a thorough job of wrecking the environment, and these new schools appeal to the idealism and sense of mission of Russia's young people. Many other former communist countries are giving birth to systems of educational choice modeled on Western Europe's, and many of the new independent schools offer religious-based instruction, in keeping with the spiritual rebirth that is taking place in these newly free countries. Many of the Eastern European delegates at the ECNAIS conference were genuinely surprised to learn that in the United States, elementary and secondary education has remained a virtual state monopoly. Several asked me why American voters would tolerate a "Soviet-style" education system. The best I could offer was that we do, at least, have freedom of choice in higher education, and we do have world-class universities.

In Western Europe, educational choice has been the norm for decades. In 1984, in fact, the European Parliament mandated that all Common Market countries offer a private school education supported by a government scholarship to all families who desire it.

In 1987 I spent a month studying Denmark's system of free choice of schools, established more than 140 years ago by the great educator N. F. S. Grundtvig. I visited schools for the disabled, for ethnic minorities, and an "international school." I remember especially a school specializing in the fine arts. Although I arrived virtually unannounced, the school was neat and clean, and the students were all busily at work. The teacher who showed me around saw my astonishment and commented, "You know, Alan, it's a joy to teach in this school, because the students have *chosen* to be here and they value what we have to offer." Where is the American public school teacher who could make the same statement?

In 1988 I spent a month in the Netherlands studying its system of educational freedom of choice, a right enshrined in its constitution. Of the many schools I visited, the most memorable was a "skipper school," devoted to the special needs of the transient children whose parents own barges that ply the Rhine and the canals of Europe. As a Spanish-speaking physician working in county hospitals, I've had many Latino migrant farm workers as patients. Among their most bitter complaints is that every time they move, they must change schools. One of my dreams is that these families will one day, with a system of freedom of schooling, be able to choose schools that address their specialized needs. Imagine if these kids had access to a system of mobile classrooms, modeled after Holland's skipper schools, with teachers trained in meeting their unique needs in language and acculturation.

One of my main impressions in Holland was the utter lack of controversy surrounding their system of freedom of choice, in effect now for over a century. I met a grand total of one Dutchman who thought his country might be better off with an American-style compulsory government school system, and even he cheerfully admitted that he'd never in his life met another Hollander who agreed with him. The closest the Dutch have come to any controversy about their fundamental values was when Islamic families grew numerous enough to demand their own school. There was initially some debate about whether the government should permit a school based on a "nontraditional" religion, but, fortunately, the Dutch commitment to freedom and tolerance won out, and in 1987 the first Islamic school opened. Today there are five.

In Spain, about a third of all children attend independent schools. The Spanish delegates at the ECNAIS conference complained that their prime minister was trying to cut back independent school funding, even though he was a product of a private school and was sending his own daughter to a private school, "just like Bill Clinton."

In France, an attempt by the government in 1984 to take away government-funded independent schools was met by the largest nationwide demonstrations in French history—larger even than the anti–Vietnam War demonstrations of the 1960s. A million and a half citizens fought for, and won, the right to keep *l'école libre.*

Nor is educational freedom of choice confined to Europe. Israel, Canada, Australia, New Zealand, and Japan all have far more freedom of choice at the elementary and secondary levels than we do in the United States. We stand alone in having such a monopolistic, centralized system. Is it merely a coincidence that we also stand at or near the bottom in all objective tests of educational outcomes, behind even some developing countries such as Korea, and that our dropout rate is among the developed world's highest?

The president of ECNAIS, Peter Mason, commented in Berlin about the unfortunate implications of American terminology regarding schools. Mason, a British intelligence officer during the Second World War, was for many years headmaster of the Manchester Grammar School and has written many books on educational freedom of choice throughout the world.

"I don't like the term 'private school' at all," he said. "It implies exclusivity and elitism, and a school that accepts students from all walks of life who bring with them their fair share of educational tax dollars is anything but that. As well, the terminology in Great Britain is the reverse of yours: in the sixteenth century, when *all* schools were private, the better private schools that accepted students from all over England became known as 'public' schools, and the name has stuck to this day. We prefer the terms 'independent school' or 'free school,' and I wish you in America would adopt the same terminology."

Even in America, the term "public school" does not always carry the same meaning that it used to. Nobody claims that the public schools of Watts provide the same quality as those of Beverly Hills. America's "public" school system is, in fact, very heavily segregated, in terms of both race and economic class—a result of our insistence on assigning students to a particular public school based on geographical residence. One need not look hard to find public school systems overseas that have had the same effect. The most extreme example is South Africa, where, under apartheid, private schools were the only integrated schools in the country.

Many Americans, shocked to see our public schools failing to supply textbooks, paper, and pencils to students, jump to the conclusion that the problem is a lack of money. In fact, however, U.S. per student expenditures rose *96 percent* in constant dollars between 1970 and 1990 and are now much higher than those of any other country in the world (see Table 5.1).

As the conference ended, we said our farewells and took leave of this extraordinary city, promising to meet again the following year in Madrid. As I caught a taxi to Berlin's Tempelhof airport, I suddenly remembered something I'd forgotten to do. I asked the driver to stop at a souvenir stand, and hurriedly bought a keepsake of my visit—a stone from the old Berlin Wall—and stuffed it in my pocket.

If the Berlin Wall could come down, I told myself, perhaps an American educational system that works isn't the impossible dream after all.

Table 5-1

Public expenditures per student for K–12 education for the school year 1991–92, in constant 1992 U.S. dollars.

Country	Dollars
United States	6,984
Sweden	5,336
Norway	5,262
Canada	4,935
Switzerland	4,838
Denmark	4,475
Finland	4,237
Austria	4,107
Italy	4,036
France	3,630
Belgium	3,438
United Kingdom	3,365
The Netherlands	3,192
Germany	3,084
Japan	2,707
Australia	2,532
New Zealand	2,263
Spain	2,094
Ireland	2,083
Hungary	1,728

Source: U.S. Department of Education, National Center for Education Statistics, 1995.

Chapter 6

The Empirical Evidence for School Choice

A new idea is first condemned as ridiculous and then dismissed as trivial, until finally, it becomes what everybody knows.

— *WILLIAM JAMES*

Defenders of the public school monopoly claim that schools of choice aren't really better and that the parents paying thousands of dollars a year from their own pockets for a better education for their children are getting little or nothing for their money. They insist that the vast differences in test scores, dropout rates, and campus violence rates between public and private schools are due not to the superiority of private schools but to the higher socioeconomic status of the children attending them and to their better home preparation for learning.

There is, in fact, some truth to these assertions. Every serious study of the predictors of academic success has pointed to the students' socioeconomic status as one of the most important, if not *the* most important, factors. Children who come from well-educated, high-income families, who are read to from an early age, and who are encouraged by their parents to excel in school tend to do well even in bad schools. And the children of poorly educated, low-income parents for whom English is a second language often have a rough time even in the best, most supportive schools.

Although many private schools, particularly Catholic parochial schools, enroll a high percentage of children from low-income families, on the whole it is undeniably true—but also, as it turns out, largely irrelevant—that children who attend private schools come from generally higher socioeconomic status families.

The debate over the source of the success of private schools raged on without definitive proof one way or the other until the 1982 publication of *High School Achievement* by the late James Coleman, Professor of Sociology at the University of Chicago, and his assistants Thomas Hoffer and Sally Kilgore.[1] Their research was based on the 1980 National Center for Education Statistics study, "High School and Beyond." Conducted by the National Opinion Research Center at the University of Chicago, this study encompassed 58,728 students in 1,015 public and private high schools. Researchers concentrated almost exclusively on Catholic schools, since these constitute the only homogeneous private school "system" in the United States. When they compared the Catholic schools with American public high schools, *with all outcomes controlled for socioeconomic status,* the results were startling and conclusive. Consider:

➤ The rate of learning in Catholic high schools was *25 to 50 percent greater* than that in public schools—a statistic that is all the more striking when one recalls that Catholic schools charge tuitions in the $2,000 range, on average, or about one-third the per student spending levels in American public schools.

➤ The Catholic schools provided a much safer, more disciplined, and more ordered environment than did the public schools.

➤ The dropout rate in the Catholic schools was much lower.

➤ The Catholic schools were as racially well integrated as the public schools.

In 1983–1984, the original "High School and Beyond" study was augmented. Both the original data and the new data were included in a report on the performance of public and private schools, including both Catholic and non-Catholic private schools, by distinguished researchers John E. Chubb and

---

[1] James S. Coleman, Thomas Hoffer, and Sally Kilgore, *High School Achievement: Public, Catholic, and Private Schools Compared* (New York: Basic Books, 1982).

Terry M. Moe, both then of the Brookings Institution. Published in 1990 as the landmark book *Politics, Markets, and America's Schools,* this study controlled for no fewer than 220 variables thought to be relevant to school performance.[2] It provided school reformers a wealth of data that supported the Coleman studies in greater detail and with more evidence. Although the results are far too complex and voluminous to summarize here, the authors themselves reported that three simple and straightforward findings stood out from their exhaustive research:

1.   Schools perform better to the extent that they have clear goals, an ambitious academic program, strong educational leadership, and high levels of teacher professionalism.

2.   The most important prerequisite for the emergence of effective school characteristics is school autonomy, especially from external bureaucratic influences.

3.   America's existing system of public education inhibits the emergence of effective organizations. This occurs because it limits and undermines school autonomy.

Quoting directly from Chubb and Moe's book,

In a market setting, principals and teachers are likely to have a great deal of discretion in determining school practices. In putting that discretion to use, they need not be driven to adopt practices whose major justification is that they avoid offending anyone. Schools can be clear, bold, and controversial in the practices they adopt as long as they attract a specialized clientele that values what they do. They are free, in particular, to adopt whatever practices they consider most suitable to the effective pursuit of the school's mission—and they have strong incentives, as we have seen, to do just that by building an organizational team that enables a school to take advantage of the expertise and judgment of its teachers.

---

[2] John E. Chubb and Terry M. Moe, *Politics, Markets, and America's Schools* (Washington, DC: The Brookings Institution, 1990).

In 1995, Terry Moe, now of the Hoover Institution at Stanford University, edited a second important academic study of school choice, this one on private choice programs and entitled simply *Private Vouchers*.[3] In 1991, J. Patrick Rooney, CEO of the Golden Rule Insurance Company, had established a private voucher program in Indiana for low-income children wishing to attend private schools. This highly successful program inspired similar ones in many other cities. As of early 1997, there are twenty-eight privately funded programs in major American cities encompassing about 10,700 low-income children. (Of the two in California, one is in Los Angeles, sponsored by John Walton of Wal-Mart and Larry Smead of SASCO Electric, and the other is in Oakland, sponsored by Ruth Berg.)

Moe's book chronicles the achievements of these visionary programs. Although none of them have been in existence longer than five years and none of the studies have yet controlled for socioeconomic status, the preliminary findings are so overwhelmingly positive that they will undoubtedly stand up to the most rigorous scrutiny. The studies show that in these private voucher programs, dropout rates have plummeted and family satisfaction has soared.

The results of school choice in the United States—not to mention the superior results of choice programs overseas—make it clear that those American parents who are digging deep into their pockets for a private school education for their children are doing so not because they enjoy throwing their money away, but because there are conclusive and quantifiable benefits in schools of choice.

And what about the true experts on the quality of America's public schools—the public school teachers themselves? Where are they sending *their* children to school?

Read on.

---

[3] Terry M. Moe, ed., *Private Vouchers* (Stanford, CA: Hoover Institution Press, 1995).

Chapter 7

Where Connoisseurs Send Their Kids

In early 1993, the National Education Association was stunned when both President Clinton and Vice President Gore, shortly after their inauguration, refused to send their own children to Washington, DC, public schools. The NEA had been not only one of the largest donors to the Clinton/Gore election campaign, but the single largest source of volunteer labor. Yet even that massive display of political muscle wasn't enough to convince Clinton and Gore to put their own loved ones in Washington's public schools—or any other public schools, for that matter.

Clinton and Gore, however, were far from alone. Of the 535 elected members of the Senate and the House of Representatives, the number who are willing to subject their own children to the dangers and dismal quality of the District of Columbia's public schools can be counted on one hand—with fingers left over. *None* of the senior administrators in the U.S. Department of Education send their own children to public schools there. Jesse Jackson, who campaigned in California against Proposition 174, the school voucher initiative, sent his own two children to Catholic parochial schools. And the list goes on.

Perhaps most telling, though, is that in America's big-city school districts, public school teachers themselves are refusing to send *their* children to the same public schools in which they work. A study by Denis P. Doyle of the Hudson Institute, based on official 1990 U.S. Census Bureau data and published under the title, "Where Connoisseurs Send Their Children to School," found that in nineteen of the twenty largest cities in the United States, the percentage of public school teachers who send their children to private schools is greater—often *much* greater—than the percentage for the general public.[1]

The data shown in Table 7.1 tell the story. Note that the table includes the four cities profiled elsewhere in this book: Milwaukee (Chapter 2) and Cleveland, Washington, DC, and Jersey City (Chapter 31).

These four cities have established, or are trying to establish, school choice programs, the strongest impetus for which has been in cities in which the schools are so bad that public school teachers send their own children to private schools at high rates. Many of those same teachers hypocritically fight school choice programs designed to benefit low-income families who can't afford private schools for their children, but who are most in need of them.

As high as the numbers in Table 7.1 are, they are much higher still for public school administrators with their six-figure salaries, although statistical proof of this awaits a definitive study. What *is* certain from Doyle's analysis is that the more teachers earn, the more likely they are to use private schools— just like the general public.

Table 7-1

Private school enrollment in some major American cities, from 1990 Census Bureau data: children of the general public compared with children of public school teachers.

City	Enrollment Rate, Children of the General Public (percent)	Enrollment Rate, Children of Public School Teachers (percent)	Difference by Which Teachers' Rate Exceeds General Public's Rate (percent)
Nationwide Except California			
Atlanta	12.6	17.9	42
Baltimore	18.1	31.7	75
Boston	28.9	44.6	54
Chicago	26.6	36.3	36
Cleveland	25.2	39.7	58
Dallas	14.1	20.8	48
Denver	17.7	26.7	51

[1] Denis P. Doyle, "Where Connoisseurs Send Their Children to School" (Washington, DC: The Center for Education Reform, 1995). Our chapter title is used with Doyle's permission.

City	Enrollment Rate, Children of the General Public (percent)	Enrollment Rate, Children of Public School Teachers (percent)	Difference by Which Teachers' Rate Exceeds General Public's Rate (percent)
Detroit	17.1	32.7	91
El Paso	7.5	12.6	68
Fort Worth	12.3	23.6	92
Honolulu	31.0	45.0	45
Houston	11.6	13.9	20
Indianapolis	16.6	23.5	42
Jersey City	34.4	50.3	46
Miami	13.2	31.4	138
Milwaukee	23.9	32.9	38
Minneapolis	19.9	24.8	25
New Orleans	26.5	38.2	44
New York	24.6	27.9	13
Newark	18.8	37.8	101
Philadelphia	34.7	35.9	3
Phoenix	10.1	12.6	25
Pittsburgh	28.0	35.4	26
Portland	14.1	21.1	50
San Antonio	11.4	19.4	70
Seattle	28.7	30.8	7
Spokane	12.3	16.1	31
Saint Louis	28.4	31.4	11
Tacoma	12.2	18.1	48
Tucson	11.2	18.0	61
Wash., DC	19.7	28.2	43

California

City	Enrollment Rate, Children of the General Public (percent)	Enrollment Rate, Children of Public School Teachers (percent)	Difference by Which Teachers' Rate Exceeds General Public's Rate (percent)
Bakersfield	9.7	15.4	59
Fresno	6.2	8.8	42
Los Angeles	19.5	30.1	54
Oakland	18.0	28.1	56
Sacramento	13.4	20.7	54
San Diego	11.8	13.0	10
San Francisco	30.1	36.7	22
San Jose	13.0	15.9	22

Source: Denis P. Doyle, "Where Connoisseurs Send Their Children to School" (Washington, DC: The Center for Education Reform, 1995). In the nation's 100 largest cities, the average private school enrollment for the general public is 13.1 percent; it is about 10 percent for the nation as a whole.

The implications of all this are obvious. As Doyle expressed it in his report,

> That teachers prefer private schools drives home arguments about choice, not in terms of competition, but in terms of its ethical and normative dimension. With teachers choosing private schools, the truth is self-evident: while they work in public schools, they choose private schools for their own children because they believe they are better. They are connoisseurs. And no one in our society is better qualified to make that judgment than teachers.

> . . . To more and more teachers, teaching is a job and school is a business; if schools were able to exert some compelling claim on our loyalty—if, for example, they were superb instruments for forging a democratic society, inculcating habits of prudence and civic virtue—we could argue that teachers *should* send their children to public school. Indeed, teachers would so argue, as they have in the past. The fact is that teachers who actually make the decision to enroll their children in private school are overcoming a strong professional push to the contrary.

> We are left, then, with a striking spectacle. By and large, it is the poor and dispossessed, particularly in large, troubled urban areas, who are forced into public schools.

Doyle concludes, "No matter how one examines the data, teachers and their organizations owe the public an answer to this question: If they reject the institutions they are teaching in and feel free to choose a private alternative, *on what basis should the poor and dispossessed be denied this option?*"

Chapter 8

Why Not Just Fix the Public Schools?

Those of us who have worked long and hard for educational choice have heard the refrain a thousand times: "Why not just fix the public schools? They used to be fine, and they could be again if we all just pulled together. If you guys spent as much time working to improve the public schools as you do pushing your voucher system, we could really get somewhere."

It has a reasonable ring to it. Public schools were undeniably much better only a few decades ago; why can't we just turn back the clock to a happier, more productive time? For those who know the public school monopoly well, the reasons why that will never happen are abundantly clear. Public schools are fundamentally different from how they were just a few decades ago, and they are different in ways that make meaningful reform from within impossible. To put it another way, you can't get there from here.

There was a time when public schools were truly locally governed. Most of the tax revenues were assessed locally, and the taxes stayed in the community. A school board was elected, and most parents knew the board members personally. The system was responsive, and problems were identified and fixed. Today, however, only a small part of public school moneys are assessed and spent locally. Most of the money is collected and spent by the states; in California, the state accounts for about 70 percent of all school spending. Another large part comes from the federal government, and county school districts make up a fourth revenue source.

The many funding sources make public school governance today a nightmare of inefficiency and crossed purposes. Most federal and state aid to education is categorical: the money, rather than simply being given to the school districts to spend on their highest priorities, is earmarked for specific purposes, however irrelevant they may be to community needs. State governance of education is divided in responsibility among the legislature, the governor's office (which in most states has its own office of education), the state school board, and the state superintendent of public instruction. Responsibility is further divided at the county and local levels. Decision making is hamstrung by a rigid educational code. California's, for example, runs to eleven volumes containing about *100,000 Sections*. No one can seriously claim to comprehend this behemoth of bureaucratic rules and regulations, which, among other things (in a concession to the janitors union), *prohibits* parents from doing volunteer maintenance on California's public schools!

If a mad political scientist had set out to design a decision-making process to be as unresponsive, unaccountable, and chaotic as possible, he might have come up with something like the system we have today. *Nobody is in charge.* There is no true responsibility or accountability for *anything*. And the countless layers of bureaucracy siphon off a huge percentage of all the tax money assessed for public schools. While the Los Angeles Unified School District pleads poverty and is unable to put pencils, paper, and up-to-date textbooks in the hands of the children, the superintendent is riding around town in a limousine driven by a chauffeur who makes more money than most teachers.

In truth, there is really a fifth layer of governance: the teachers unions, which are much more powerful today than they once were. The California Teachers Association is by far the largest, wealthiest, and most powerful political lobby in the state. It is very difficult to be elected to a school board without union financing and support. California's Superintendent of Public Instruction, Delaine Eastin, owes her *entire political career* to money from the CTA, putting California in the absurd position of having a superintendent who is not so much the supervisor of our teachers as their employee. The fox is guarding the chicken coop.

Another factor in the decline of public schools is the vast increase in the number of administrative and other nonteaching personnel (see Figure 8.1).

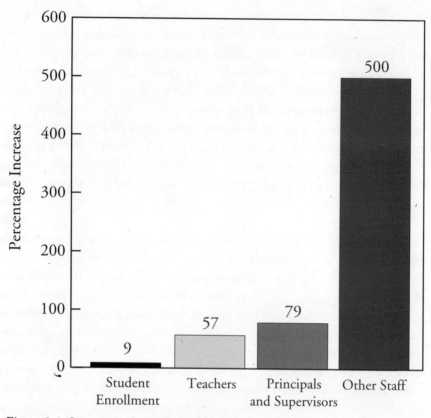

Figure 8.1 *Increase in American public school enrollment vs. that of school personnel, 1960–1984. [From David Boaz, "The Public School Monopoly: America's Berlin Wall," in David Boaz, ed.,* Liberating Schools: Education in the Inner City *(Washington, DC: Cato Institute, 1991), 16.]*

During the 1950s, about 80 percent of all employees in American public schools were teachers; today, there isn't a big-city school district in the nation in which teachers are even a majority of the employees. Many administrators are grossly overpaid, often pulling down six-figure salaries, so they have an extraordinary incentive to protect their positions and their perks. Through their unions, such as the Association of California School Administrators, they have become a special interest group of their own, keeping the schools firmly mired in the status quo. This army of civil servants seems ever intent on proving the truth of Honoré de Balzac's observation that "Bureaucracies are giant mechanisms operated by pygmies."

As if this nightmare of a system weren't bad enough by itself, our nation's public schools have become so discredited that it is increasingly difficult to get good people to work in them. Although there are still some exceptionally bright and motivated individuals going into teaching for idealistic reasons, most credentialed public school teachers entering the system today are coming from the bottom third of their college classes. Among this group, the failure rate on the CBEST exam—a test of tenth-grade skills—is shockingly high (see sidebar). Sadly, this bears out a prediction made in 1989 by the late Albert Shanker, president of the American Federation of Teachers: ". . . [in the 1990s] we're going to be digging even deeper, and the teachers are going to be even dumber."

The result of this morass is a public school system utterly incapable of reform—and it's getting worse every year. Even the most brilliant, well-intentioned, energetic superintendent of public instruction can't effect any meaningful change in a system so insulated from the results of its failures and so haphazardly structured as to leave it with no accountability. Recruiting the "best people" hasn't worked; some highly capable and energetic people have been put in charge of various state and big-city public school systems recently, sometimes with great fanfare, but always with disappointing results. If it were possible to reform the existing public school system from within, wouldn't someone, somewhere in the United States, have done it by now? Yet there are no success stories anywhere in the nation. Public school teachers and administrators in many states are well aware that they face the specter of new competition from school choice systems, a subject they discuss among themselves at length. But even this perceived threat to their livelihoods has not translated into any substantive improvements in the public schools.

What *has* worked to improve public schools is freedom of choice and open competition. Just as UC Berkeley keeps its standards high because of fierce competition from Stanford, and the USC medical school keeps UCLA's medical school on its toes, educational choice will improve our public schools. Of the two countries that are culturally most similar to the United States—Australia and Canada—both have established school choice systems within the last twenty years. Australia's is primarily in New South Wales and Victoria, and Canada's is primarily in British Columbia. There is essentially no controversy in those countries about the obvious improvement in public school quality that resulted from the new competition and freedom of choice.

When public school teachers and administrators alike can see families voting with their feet and leaving for higher-quality neighborhood schools of choice, they will get the message pronto that their consumers want higher standards, with more money for the classrooms and less for administrators. Just as the U.S. Postal Service, slug that it was, improved when Federal Express came along, a dose of good old American free enterprise will light a much-needed fire under the public schools.

Imagine what it would mean if our low-income and minority families could confront those school officials and say, "Either do what it takes to make this campus a safe enough place that you'd enroll your own child here, or I'm taking my voucher and enrolling my daughter in the new neighborhood school down the street." Imagine what it will be like for these families to be able at last to get in the face of those bureaucrats—and make them an offer they can't refuse.

The CBEST Examination

All applicants for teacher credentialing in California and Oregon must pass the California Basic Educational Skills Test (CBEST). Although state education officials deny it, it is commonly understood to be geared to about a tenth-grade (if that) proficiency level in reading, writing, and mathematics. This raises a question: *Why are college graduates who wish to be teachers (perhaps even of the eleventh or twelfth grade) required to demonstrate no more than a high school sophomore's proficiency in these most "basic educational skills"?*

The reading and math tests are all multiple choice (50 questions each), with no penalty for incorrect answers; the writing test consists of two essay questions. All three tests are scored on a sliding scale from 20 to 80; the passing score on each test is 41, but it is possible to pass overall with a scaled score as low as 37 on one or two sections. To pass, one must answer only slightly more than half (about 55 percent) of the questions correctly. In other words, abysmal scores that would traditionally have rated an *F* in school will get you through the CBEST.

Following are some sample questions taken from the "CBEST 1996–1997 Registration Bulletin."[1]

Read the passages below; then answer the questions that follow them.

4. The Great Depression of the 1930s in the United States accelerated a trend in the field of education already underway—the rise in educational standards for teachers. The difficulty of finding jobs encouraged prospective teachers to stay in school longer; school districts could now insist that teachers have a college degree, often without raising salaries or improving working conditions.

Based on the information in the passage, which of the following is a true statement about trends in education during the Great Depression in the United States?

A. College degree programs increased their requirements.

B. Standards of education for teachers rose because jobs were scarce.

C. School districts encouraged teachers to accept lower salaries.

D. Prospective teachers insisted on improved working conditions.

E. Working conditions declined as educational standards increased.

5. After touring the plains toward the close of the cowboy era, journalist Richard Harding Davis observed, "The inhabited part of a ranch, the part of it on which the owners live, bears about the same proportion to the rest of the ranch as a lighthouse does to the ocean around it."

Based on Richard Harding Davis's observation, which of the following can be inferred about a ranch toward the close of the cowboy era?

---

[1] Readers may request a free copy of this revealing document (and obtain the answers to the questions) by writing to CBEST Program, National Evaluation Systems, Inc., P.O. Box 340880, Sacramento, CA 95834–0880; or call (916) 928–4001.

A. Most of a ranch was uninhabited by its owners.

B. The size of a ranch rivaled the size of an ocean.

C. Inhabitants of a ranch typically lived in privacy and seclusion.

D. The working area around a ranch was uninhabitable by humans.

E. The inhabitants of a ranch, like those of a lighthouse, should be viewed as caretakers.

15. All fruit juices contain the sugar fructose, and there is no doubt that some kinds of sugar are harmful.

Which of the following can be correctly inferred from the statement above?

A.   All fruit juices are harmful.

B.   Some, but not all, fruit juices are harmful.

C.   Grapefruit juice does not contain any sugar.

D.   Fruit juices are more harmful than vegetable juices.

E.   Orange juice contains at least one kind of sugar.

21. Amy drinks 1½ cups of milk three times a day. At this rate, how many cups of milk will she drink in one week?

A.   4 ½

B.   7 ½

C.   10 ½

D.   21 ½

E.   31 ½

24. Which of the following methods could be used to solve the problem below?

The moon is about 238,000 miles from the earth, and the sun is about 93,000,000 miles from the earth. The sun is about how many times as far from the earth as the moon is?

A. Multiply 238,000 by 93,000,000.

B. Divide 93,000,000 by 238,000.

C. Add 238,000 and 93,000,000.

D. Subtract 238,000 from 93,000,000.

E. Divide 238,000 by 93,000,000.

34. Of the five types of dogs listed below, which type eats the LEAST amount of food?

Collies eat more than basset hounds. Boxers eat more than collies. Beagles eat more than basset hounds, but less than collies. Boxers eat less than dalmatians.

A. collie

B. basset hound

C. boxer

D. beagle

E. dalmatian

39. Which of the following figures does NOT have at least one pair of parallel sides?

A.

B.

C.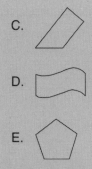

D.

E.

Applicants are given four hours to wrestle with these mind benders, and there is no limit to the number of times they may take the test in order to pass—nor is it even necessary to pass all three sections at the same time!

In the *San Francisco Chronicle* of February 23, 1996, Debra Saunders reported that an official of the California Commission on Teacher Credentialing—the man responsible, in fact, for defending the test against teachers who complain that it's too difficult—had given the test to his eleven-year-old triplet daughters, and all three passed with perfect scores.

In 1992, three teachers associations sued on behalf of the *50,000 applicants* who had failed the test, to have it invalidated on the basis that it is "discriminatory." In September 1996, a U.S. district court ruled that anyone hoping to teach in California's public schools must still pass a basic skills test. The three teachers associations have vowed to appeal.

Chapter 9

A View from Inside

James Horsman

I am often asked, "Isn't teaching difficult?" My response, after the Cheshire cat grin sweeps across my face, is, "Surely you're joking? I make $50,000 per year with fourteen weeks vacation, I get off work at three o'clock, and my salary doesn't go down if I do my job badly. After all, when was the last time you heard of the government's underpaying for anything?" The response I usually get is, "I see your point."

But in a more important sense than money, teaching in an American public school is *not* the rewarding, uplifting occupation it could be and should be. None of my students get to choose their teachers—let alone the school itself. They're there because they *have* to be, not because they *want* to be. If a student thought that he or she could get a better education from another teacher—or at another school—that's just too bad. It is not unlike walking into your neighborhood restaurant, ordering a steak, and being told, "We've decided that liver is what you'll eat today."

My school doesn't get to choose its students, either. Many believe that this is as it should be, but this belief is based on the fallacy that *any* public school should be capable of educating *any* child to his or her fullest potential. There is not a restaurant in America that specializes in everything, believing that everyone within driving distance is going to enjoy its cuisine. Why should schools and teachers think differently?

Some people ask, "What difference does the teacher make? They all teach the same, don't they? In a word, no. Teachers have the latitude to do almost

53

anything they want for instruction (what to emphasize, what homework to assign, etc.) and grading. Any teacher can give any grade to any child for any reason. One English teacher at my school, under the guise of upholding standards, routinely fails about 70 percent of her students, including *all* of my basic math students (who, by definition, are not good students; the better students take other math courses). The students, knowing that the deck is stacked, soon give up even trying.

Of course, once in a while a student or parent will demand that you justify a low grade, but I have never heard of a teacher's being asked to justify a *high* grade. Most teachers seek to minimize disharmony in the class by giving high grades. That is why so many students get passed from one grade to the next and finally graduate as functional illiterates.

I am always amazed by the faith parents have that grades are an accurate measure of their child's academic achievement. I remember the first college-bound class I taught. They were hard-working, pleasant, low-income, minority students from an urban school. They were shocked when I wrote their test results from the math section of the PSAT on the board. Their median score was in the *ninth* percentile, meaning that 91 percent of children around the country had done better than they did on the exam. All their lives, people had been telling them how good they were. And they *were,* compared with those around them—but *not* compared with a much larger cohort. None had any idea that they were not among the smartest teens in the country.

In February of 1987, I was assigned to teach my first calculus class. Because I had a burning desire to become a superior teacher, and because I had not been very successful thus far, I decided to visit Garfield High School's legendary calculus teacher, Jaime Escalante, made famous by the movie *Stand and Deliver.* After all, he had already accomplished what I *hoped* to accomplish with my students at Manual Arts High. He had taught a bunch of minority teenagers, whom everyone else had written off as incorrigible, unteachable anti-intellectuals, to pass the advanced placement (AP) calculus exam.

I drove over to Garfield after work one day and dropped in on my future mentor. "I have this new calculus class," I said. "Do you have any advice for me?" He was a bit startled by my brashness, but he smiled warmly as he started to hand me course outlines, study sheets, and a stack of old quizzes and exams. We began talking—or rather, I listened while he explained how he went through a class, a day, a chapter, and a year. He emphasized *ganas* (meaning *you earn, you win,* or *you gain* in Spanish), and review, review, review. I was enthralled. I knew I could do it with the help of my new friend.

Success came slowly but surely. In my first year, only Eusavio passed. I received a note from the principal congratulating me on getting him through the exam—the first student to pass AP calculus in the sixty-year history of the school. The following year, six passed, and seven the year after that. Finally, in my fourth year, seventeen students passed. I was on top of the world. For the first time in my life, I felt that I had done something great.

The next calculus class was even better, and I had dreams of Hollywood making a movie about my teaching abilities. But I forgot one thing. In a huge school bureaucracy, everyone has their own little goals and separate agendas, and academic excellence is not even in the top ten. Despite AP calculus scores that were virtually unmatched by other inner-city schools, and despite hundreds of letters from students expressing heartfelt appreciation for how much I had done to change their lives, the principal succumbed to pressure by other teachers and a few innocuous (my opinion, not his) complaints about my unorthodox teaching style. He removed me from the program I had built and loved, and I was subsequently transferred to another high school.

During my rise to glory, not one person ever came and asked, "Gee, how did you do it?" No one from the district office came by to observe my class or ask, "Why are so many kids passing AP calculus under your tutelage while students at other schools languish in algebra or basic math?" Again, academic excellence was never one of the goals. Trying to replicate successful programs was not something anyone had time for.

What would happen at McDonald's if a manager tried something different that drastically increased profits? He would earn more money, and his technique would soon spread to every franchise in the world. Other restaurants would copy this new technique as soon as they could figure it out.

By contrast, dissemination of new, useful, proven instructional practices rarely occurs in public schools, because of one simple fact: *every teacher gets paid the same as every other teacher who has the same tenure.* The district doesn't care about knowing which teachers are excellent and which are laggards. If teachers draw attention to themselves by outstanding achievements, they only incur the ire of their colleagues, who justify their collective exasperation and inability to teach their own students by blaming the students, their parents, and their neighborhoods. A *successful* teacher only exposes the cult of excuses as a myth and a lie.

Another question I am asked is, "What *do* students learn in school?" The fact is, almost all children in public schools learn two things: The first is how to be dependent on someone else as their source of knowledge. Teachers encourage this. It is easiest to control a class if everyone is doing the same activity, so you explain to the students that they are to do only what you, the teacher, tell them to do. After a few years of this browbeating, even the most independent-minded youngsters learn that their optimal strategy, the path of least resistance, is just to go along to get along.

The second thing children learn is how to hate learning. At my school, every ninth-grader is required to read Charles Dickens's *Great Expectations.* If you were a bad student with poor reading skills in the ninth grade, and you didn't like to read, would there be any way for someone to bring that book to life? I doubt it. Think about it: every child, whether he or she wants to be an English professor or a truck driver, must read that book. Again, this is the same as walking into a restaurant hoping for your favorite meal and being served liver, because that is what the restaurant prefers you to have.

Consider the difference between the typical five-year-old, just starting school, and the typical fifteen-year-old after he or she has been incarcerated in mandatory child care institutions for ten years. Virtually all five-year-olds love to read. Perhaps 2 percent of fifteen-year-olds share this love; they are usually the ones who march to a different drummer and haven't succumbed to the enormous pressure to sit down and be quiet. Equally distressing is the lack of *curiosity* in the typical fifteen-year-old compared with a five-year-old. How many of the former ask (or can answer), "Why is the sky blue? Why are leaves green?" After being beaten down for ten years, most just give in or give up.

We will never fully tap the potential intellectual energy and vigor that lie within all children as long as we maintain the current public school monopoly. Excellence and achievement on behalf of the clients are never valued in a government bureaucracy. Job protection, self-enrichment, and the status quo are the supreme goals of the people managing the institutions I've taught in for the past thirteen years. In that, they are not dissimilar to those who ran—and ultimately brought down—the Soviet Union.

The students and their parents are the ones who deserve real sympathy, not the teachers. I'll just keep on going with my $50,000-a-year job (not counting health care benefits, etc.) with fourteen weeks vacation, shaking my head in amazement and disgust.

Chapter 10

The Phantom "Cutbacks"

One of the most frustrating challenges school choice advocates face is the persistent misconception that there have been "cutbacks" in educational funding at the elementary and secondary levels. It's obvious where this belief comes from: when people see decaying schools with broken windows and hear about schoolchildren struggling with out-of-date textbooks, it's natural to jump to the conclusion that we're spending less money now than when America's public schools were much better.

Yet the truth is that spending for elementary and secondary education in the United States, adjusted for inflation, is at a record level (in California it is at a near-record level). From 1970 to 1990, U.S. per student spending in constant (inflation-adjusted) dollars increased by *96 percent* (see Figure 10.1). In California, per student spending in constant dollars increased by 132 percent from the 1959–60 school year to the 1992–93 school year, according to Lance Izumi of the Pacific Research Institute. A June 1993 article in the *California Journal,* the prestigious, nonpartisan observer of California politics, pegged the increase from 1983 (the *A Nation at Risk* year) to 1993 alone at 13 percent, again in constant dollars.

The rapidly increasing cost of health care has received enormous attention in the American news media. Yet the far greater rate of increase in per student spending for elementary and secondary education in the United States has been almost totally ignored. While the higher spending on health care has been accompanied by improved outcomes, the higher spending on education has coincided with *declining* outcomes (see Figure 10.2).

Nor has anyone ever shown a clear correlation between per student expenditures and academic outcomes. Economist Eric Hanushek of the University of Rochester, in a study reported in *Educational Researcher*, May 1989, reviewed *sixty-five* studies of the relationship between expenditures and outcomes and found that only twenty of the studies showed any correlation at all. Several even showed an *inverse* correlation, with improved outcomes in the lower-spending schools. This quirk in the statistics is probably due to the academic excellence of America's Catholic parochial schools, which are by far our least expensive schools.

Even a glance at the raw data from the U.S. Department of Education, compiled by California legislative consultant Roger Magyar in his excellent booklet, *Can Parents be Trusted?* confirms this conclusion.[1] Of the four highest-spending states—New Jersey, Alaska, New York, and Connecticut, all of which spent between $8,000 and $10,000 per student per year in 1991–92—New Jersey and New York have consistently below-average outcomes (Alaska

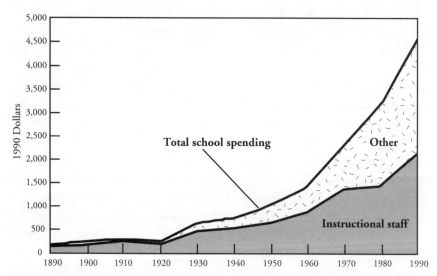

Figure 10.1 *Real current expenditure per student for K–12 education in the United States, 1890–1990, in 1990 dollars. [From Eric A. Hanushek and Steven D. Rivkin, "Understanding the 20th Century Explosion in U.S. School Costs," Working Paper 388 (Rochester, NY: Rochester Center for Economic Research, 1994).]*

---

[1] Roger Magyar, *Can Parents Be Trusted?* 1993. Available from Roger Magyar, P.O. Box 160637, Sacramento, CA 95816. He can be reached at (916) 444–8725.

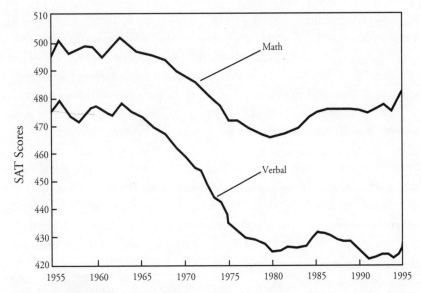

Figure 10.2 Scholastic Aptitude Test results in the United States, 1955–1995. (Source: *College Entrance Examination Board.*)

is somewhat above average, and Connecticut is average); by contrast, the *lowest*-spending state, Utah, is near the top in outcomes. It is also revealing that, although New York, for example, spends almost twice as much per student as California (which ranks thirty-six on the list), its SAT scores are lower and its dropout rate is higher.

One of the highest-spending political entities in the United States isn't a state at all, but the District of Columbia, which, if it *were* a state, would rank fifth in per student spending. Yet Washington's public schools are so deplorable that even politicians who owe their entire political careers to the National Education Association won't enroll their own children there. School officials are currently considering placing armed guards in the hallways because school violence is so rampant. Only 63 percent of the District of Columbia's public school students graduate, and a 1994 study by the U.S. Department of Education found that *78 percent* of fourth-graders there could not read.

Surely the most important reason for the lack of correlation between public school expenditures and academic outcomes is the extraordinary growth of the "Blob"—the public school bureaucracy that can be so consistently counted on to watch out for itself at the expense of the nation's children. Public school expenditures are filtered through *five* different levels of administration—federal, state, county, local, and school-site—each of which takes its cut before a single dollar ever reaches the classroom. The Los Angeles Unified School District (LAUSD) even has a sixth level, "regional administrators," who absorb about 10 million dollars of tax money per year. The county school districts, in particular, should be singled out as redundant; their job is exclusively paper pushing, and almost nothing they do directly benefits any children.

In 1990, the United Teachers–Los Angeles published a report demonstrating that 31 percent of expenditures in the LAUSD were absorbed by the central and regional administrative offices alone (see sidebar). In a blistering denunciation of the administrative bloat and waste, the report observed that "If the taxpayers of Los Angeles knew how their money was being spent, they would demand a complete cleanup."[2]

A study by Santa Monica's RAND Corporation in 1995 demonstrated that in California, only about 70 percent of all educational tax dollars actually reached the schools at all. Of this amount, another 9 percent was spent on administration within the school itself, leaving only 61 percent that trickled down to actually help the children. Even this figure, however, overstates the true level of classroom spending, for two reasons.

First, the RAND study included only state, county, and district spending. When the overhead at the federal level is factored in, the proportion of tax dollars devoted to classroom spending drops another 4 percent, leaving only 57 percent of educational tax moneys finding their way through the classroom door. Second, the RAND study arrived at the above figures simply by examining the books of the state of California and various school districts, since the funding for the study was inadequate to pay for investigators to actually track expenditures. But public school insiders know that a favorite way of school districts to mask administrative expenses is to list anyone with a teaching credential as a teacher, *even if they are employed as administrators.* Many school reformers, including the authors of this book, believe that when this subterfuge is factored in, *less than half of all educational tax money is actually directed to the needs of schoolchildren.*

---

[2] This amazing report was unearthed by prominent taxpayer activist Mike Ford, one of the prime movers in both the California term limits initiative (Prop. 140 in 1990) and the school voucher initiative (Prop. 174 in 1993).

What this means is that a voucher system that gives families a voucher worth, say, two-thirds of per student public school spending will actually *increase* direct classroom spending for those families, since schools of choice are invariably more responsive to the needs of their families and devote more of their resources to the classroom—an especially important factor for states, such as California, that are being squeezed financially.

In California we are faced not only with a dramatic increase in public school enrollment as a result of the "mini–Baby Boom" of late-blooming Boomers having their own kids (as well as many immigrant families having more children than established resident families), but also with budget pressures as a result of soaring Medi-Cal costs and prison construction. A U.S. Department of Education report released in August 1996 showed that, while public school enrollments will increase nationwide by 15 percent between now and the year 2006, California faces a larger hit than any other state, with a projected 17.8 percent increase. Thus, the only "solution" the public school establishment has proposed—spending more money without any accountability—hasn't worked in California, hasn't worked in any other state, and couldn't happen even if we wanted it to, because it will be a struggle just to keep per student spending levels as high as they are now. We *must* spend smarter, because we *can't* spend more.

Of course, there's no question that expenditures on resources such as science labs, musical instruments, computers, and athletic facilities produce educational outcomes that can't be measured with pencil-and-paper tests, and the authors of this book are not opposed to higher educational spending in principle. But, as John Chubb and Terry Moe have demonstrated, what consistently produces better educational outcomes is *not money*, but rather the *autonomy* that allows schools to be responsive to the needs of their clients. Autonomy demands strong leadership, of course, and it is made possible by school choice.

As frustrating as the voters' belief in the myth of public school spending "cutbacks" is their misperception that private schools cost several times as much as they really do. The popular image of private schools is that of the elite, exclusive country club school in which the kids wear monogrammed blazers and the yearly tuition bills rival the price of a new car. In fact, however, only about 2 percent of all private schools fall into that category. About 85 percent

of private schools are religious, and almost all of them are extraordinary bar-
gains. Many of the secular private schools are low-cost alternatives, such as
Montessori or Waldorf schools, almost all of which charge less than $5,000
per year.

The nationwide average annual tuitions for private schools, according to
1990 Census Bureau data, are shown in Figure 10.3 in comparison with the
average per student spending by the public schools in that year. The Catholic
schools have about 50 percent of the nation's private school enrollment, which
accounts for the low overall average tuition in American private schools. It is
noteworthy that about 15 percent of their students, overall, are non-Catholic;
the percentage tends to be much higher in the inner-city schools and lower in
rural areas.

Data for California alone are not easy to obtain; the best study, ironically,
was the Southwest Regional Laboratories study of 1993, commissioned by the

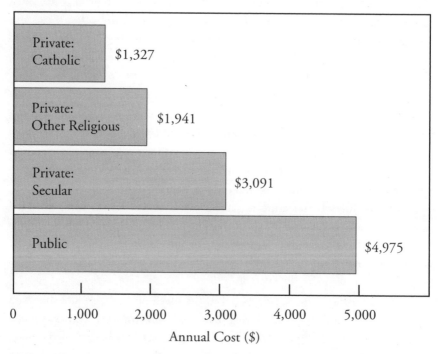

Figure 10.3 *Average annual per student costs, in 1990 dollars, for private and
public schools in the United States.* (Source: *U.S. Census Bureau.*)

anti–Proposition 174 campaign to show how expensive private schools were. In a gratifying turn of poetic justice, the authors came to the *opposite* conclusion: that the $2,600 voucher provided by the initiative was sufficient to pay the tuition at 80 percent of California's private schools. The pro-174 side used this study to good advantage, demonstrating one way to succeed with an underfunded campaign: when you don't have enough money to pay for the studies you need, use your opponents' studies against them!

One of the reasons private schools are so inexpensive is that they spend their money on teaching, not paper pushing. For example, in California's Catholic schools, 90 percent of the employees are teachers. By contrast, California doesn't have a single big-city public school district in which teachers are even a majority of the employees.

Of course, one of the main reasons why misconceptions about spending levels in public and private schools are so widespread is that the public school establishment has been so adept at perpetuating them. When California Superintendent of Public Instruction Delaine Eastin is asked in public forums about the state's per student spending level, she quotes the amount spent by the *state only,* conveniently leaving out federal, county, and local spending— thus dramatically misrepresenting the true spending levels. She then often adds that California's "dirty little secret" is that we have fallen in the state rankings from one of the higher-spending to one of the lower-spending states. While this is true enough on the surface, the impression she creates is that spending levels have fallen, when, in fact, the *real* "dirty little secret" is that they have actually *risen* dramatically and are now near an all-time record—at a time when California's educational outcomes have never been worse.

In terms of *per classroom* spending—which could be considered a more rational measure of funding levels than per student spending—it turns out that California is near the *top* of the state rankings—largely as a result of the California Teachers Association's massive clout in securing high salaries and benefits for its members. As shown by Roger Magyar in the booklet cited above, California ranked *fifth* in the nation in per classroom spending in 1991– 92, behind the same four highest-spending states mentioned earlier. Significantly, high-performing Utah was still a very low spender by this measure, ranking thirty-seventh.

Eastin also misrepresents private school spending. In public forums, she has stated that the typical California private school charges $8,000 to $10,000 per year—more than three times the true average tuition levels—an astounding display of either ignorance or dishonesty on the part of someone who claims to serve the public. One of the most deplorable deceptions of both Eastin and the California Teachers Association has been to quote the average tuitions of schools in the California Association of Independent Schools, implying that this is an umbrella organization for all of California's private schools. In fact, however, CAIS is the organization for California's elite college prep schools, representing only that 2 percent of the most expensive private schools— few of which have ever shown much interest in participating in a school choice program anyway.

Unfortunately, these are far from the only falsehoods being disseminated by California's public school establishment. On May 31, 1996, *San Francisco Chronicle* columnist Debra Saunders documented that in the San Francisco Unified School District, reports of campus violence fell by 86 percent from the 1991–92 school year to the 1994–95 school year—not because there was any *actual* decrease in crime, but because school officials had passed the word to stop reporting violent incidents. School test scores throughout the state are often reported as a percentile of other, "comparable" schools, such that, as in Garrison Keillor's Lake Wobegon, all of the children are above average. And when the Scholastic Aptitude Test was "recentered" in 1994, school districts in California and throughout the nation trumpeted the "increases" they had posted in SAT scores—without bothering to inform parents that the new, inflated scores were not comparable to the old ones.

The misrepresentations of California's dropout rates could easily be the subject of another entire chapter. In 1991, California's watchdog Little Hoover Commission found that the state was dramatically—and deliberately—understating school dropout rates. The disinformation begins with the "official" definition of the high school dropout rate, which includes only those students who have begun the tenth grade. Thus, those who drop out in the ninth grade or below *are not counted at all*. Only about 4 percent of all dropouts occur at such low grade levels, but they are all the more important because kids who leave school with such grossly inadequate education can be counted on to wind up on welfare or in prison—or in an ER, OD'd on drugs or bleeding to death from knife or gunshot wounds. There is no logical reason whatever for excluding these kids from the state's dropout statistics, except from the point of view of education bureaucrats who would rather not have the public know what is going on.

The "official" definition of the dropout rate is also skewed by counting only students who enroll in a particular grade and then leave school before completing it. Thus, a tenth-grader who drops out over the summer and never enrolls in the eleventh grade will not show up in the California Department of Education's Alice-in-Wonderland statistics.

Partly underlying the wildly inaccurate statistics the state of California disseminates is the method of collecting the data. The state, it turns out, simply asks the school districts to submit their dropout rates, and the state Department of Education uncritically accepts them, no matter how implausible they may be. Among the most serious offenders is the Oakland school district, one of the nation's worst (and the site of the notorious Ebonics farce in 1996). For years it has been fraudulently claiming dropout rates below the state average—figures that are perhaps one-third or even one-quarter of the true rates. A few rural counties have even claimed in some years to have had *no* high school dropouts—and the state Department of Education bought their story.

For 1995, the California Department of Education claimed a dropout rate of 13.5 percent. For the same year, however, the authoritative National Center for Education Statistics found California's dropout rate to be greater than 30 percent. The CDE's statistics are not even internally consistent: California's official high school graduation rate for the school year 1994–95 school year was 65.7 percent. Voters might well ask by what new math an official high school dropout rate of 13.5 percent can be reconciled with an official graduation rate of 65.7 percent.

Some of the information being put forth by our educational establishment, both nationwide and in California, is so fraudulent, and so totally implausible to those knowledgeable about public schools, that it resembles nothing so much as the inflated statistics of the old Soviet Union about the glorious "success" of each five-year plan. Perhaps, much like the welcome collapse of the Soviet empire, we will soon see the day when even the public school bureaucrats can no longer live with their own falsehoods, and the children who have been held captive by our deteriorating public school monopoly will be handed their ticket to freedom: a voucher.

Numbers Don't Lie; Fat Cats Do

In 1990, a study by the United Teachers–Los Angeles union ferreted out the interesting fact that the Los Angeles Unified School District was spending an astounding 31 percent of its entire budget on the central and regional administrative offices *alone.* These findings were reported in the February 9, 1990, issue of the house organ of the labor union, *United Teacher,* in a lead article entitled "Numbers Don't Lie; Fat Cats Do" by the then president of UTLA, Wayne Johnson.

When Johnson added up all the numbers, he was appalled to find that a total of $1,027,500,000 ($1.03 *billion*) was being spent on these non-school-based administrative expenses. His righteous indignation about how the children were being cheated of a better future came through loud and clear in his article.

"This is going to infuriate you," Johnson wrote. "It will also shock and disgust you. . . . in a district with 600,000 students and a budget of $3.5 billion, the people in charge spent only 2% on books and supplies for kids and 6% for certificated administrators' salaries. The district spends 36% of its budget on teachers' salaries plus textbooks and supplies. The question then should be asked: What is the remaining 64% of the budget spent on that is more important than teachers and books and supplies for kids?

"$1,027,500,000 was spent on running the offices at 450 North Grand and the Region Administrative Offices," Johnson continued. "This figure does not include any administration costs actually on school campuses. That $1,027,500,000 to run non-school-based administrative offices comes to 31% of the total budget.[3]

---

[3] This figure also does not include the cost of the bureaucracies at the federal, state, and county levels, all of which take their cut before the local districts see a penny of their money. Readers who would like a photocopy of the original *United Teacher* article may receive one by sending a stamped, self-addressed envelope to Dr. Alan Bonsteel, 2291 Stockton St. #407, San Francisco, CA 94133.

"Almost one-third of the District's $3.5 billion budget was spent on people who never see a kid—and they spent only $83 million on textbooks and supplies for kids!" Johnson fumed. "That is a whopping 2% for the direct educational needs of kids. . . . A district with a $3.5 billion budget that spends only 36% of it on teachers and textbooks and supplies for kids but spends 31% on the ultra-elite administrative level which never sees a kid is mismanaged beyond belief.

"Not only did the District spend its money improperly," an incredulous Johnson continued, but "while crying poverty, the fat cats actually didn't even spend all they might have. The District on July 1, 1989, had a $1,229,160,253 [$1.23 *billion*] surplus. With surpluses like these . . . they want to "freeze" the little bit of money schools have to purchase educational needs for children. They are harassing school councils by drying up even the lottery funds, which parents hoped would help their kids.

"The District fat cats . . . are still riding in taxpayer-paid-for cars, driven by taxpayer-paid-for chauffeurs," Johnson revealed. "They are still handing out phony numbers and wailing pitifully about poverty.

"A total overhaul and reform is urgently needed," Johnson urged. "If the taxpayers of Los Angeles knew how their money was being spent, they would demand a complete cleanup. It is our duty to get the information to the public."

Glad to be of help, Wayne.

Chapter 11

The Shadow Government of Our Public Schools

Carlos A. Bonilla

In 1973 Anthony Alvarado, then superintendent of the East Harlem district in the New York City public school system, introduced the free-market principle into education's huge, cumbersome, and unresponsive monopoly. Simply stated: If your business does not attract consumers, it will fail.

The East Harlem district had the lowest reading scores among the city's thirty-two school districts, and one of the lowest graduation rates: only *7 percent* of freshmen entering the district's Benjamin Franklin High School graduated. Alvarado's formula for creating an educational free market to reverse this dismal state of affairs consisted of three radical prescriptions:

1. Allow individual teachers to create whole new curricula, centered around environmental studies, the performing arts, bilingual education, or whatever best serves the needs and desires of the student body.

2. Allow students to choose among teachers and their curricula—with their parents' permission—in the same way consumers choose movies, restaurants, soap, and anything else that competing suppliers offer the public.

3. Close down any program that fails to attract enough students to sustain it.

The results of Alvarado's bold experiment in freedom of choice were dramatic:

➤ Dozens of "schools within schools" were created, all operating outside the traditional framework of stifling bureaucratic regulations.

➤ By 1984, reading scores in the district had risen well above the city's median, and 50 percent of the pupils were reading above grade average. And the graduation rate soared.

➤ Many East Harlem district students now attend the city's elite high schools and go on to colleges and universities.

Did the educational establishment hail Alvarado as an inspired innovator? Did they rush to expand and improve on such a successful program? Of course not. He was branded a maverick, one of those "freethinkers" the system should beware of, lest others follow his example and rock the comfortable boat with crazy ideas. Let students and teachers make their own decisions? Ridiculous, unheard of, preposterous!

Almost a quarter of a century after the founding of this program, and with overwhelming evidence of its success now in hand, not one other New York City school district has taken advantage of what the East Harlem experience has to offer. While opposition to reform has come at all levels of the public school establishment, the strongest opposition has come from the teachers unions. Why? *Because freedom of choice in education threatens their ability to collect union dues.*

The late Albert Shanker, president of the American Federation of Teachers, argued that ". . . parents and students won't make the right choices . . . people don't choose on the basis of educational excellence. They'll choose a school because it has a good ball team or because 'my girlfriend goes there.'" Yet Shanker didn't seem to think much of the choices being made *for* parents and students in our public schools. Never afraid to speak the truth as he saw it—no matter how painful it might be—he said, "Ninety-five percent of high school graduates cannot write a two-to-three-page letter expressing several ideas without mistakes in grammar or spelling." There is a reason for this, of course, and Shanker himself expressed it memorably: ". . . *half of those about to graduate from high school cannot even do what NAEP [National Assessment of Educational Progress] calls seventh-grade work. . . . we've known this for over twenty years. "*

With such candid admissions of the public schools' abject failure to educate our children adequately, let alone well, the vehement opposition to meaningful reform by the educational establishment is all the more disgraceful and disheartening. Keith Geiger, former president of the National Education Association, has said, "School choice will Balkanize the entire country." Yet he hasn't told us how we have benefited from the fragmentation and polarization of our society that have resulted from forcing inner-city Latino and African-American children to attend the worst public schools, many of which are quagmires of violence and despair.

The National Education Association (NEA) is the largest union in the nation (indeed, the world), having surpassed the Teamsters in the early 1990s. The NEA and its smaller rival, the American Federation of Teachers (AFT), were once professional associations dedicated to improving teaching standards. Over the last quarter-century, however, they have devolved into labor unions that have not only won the right to strike in most states, but have become profoundly influential in running our public schools—in most states now being the largest donors to partisan politics. As one local union boss put it, "We're the thousand-pound gorilla of American politics."

Unlike federal government unions, teachers unions are not subject to Hatch Act restrictions on political activity; and with mandatory dues in the NEA averaging more than $400 per year, there is plenty of money available for political lobbying (see the sidebar, "The Educartel Lobby"). A June 7, 1993, article in *Forbes* magazine estimated 1992 national NEA political action committee spending at $6.5 million, and state and local spending at $16 million. The latter amount jumped the following year as the NEA and the California Teachers Association (CTA) poured about $24 million into defeating California's school voucher initiative, Proposition 174. These figures are independent of "in-kind" spending, such as volunteer work, that is not subject to mandatory reporting. The NEA and its affiliate unions have long been the most important source of such political activities as phone banks on behalf of politicians at all levels of government.

The Educartel Lobby

According to figures supplied by the California secretary of state, various entities representing California's public elementary and secondary schools spent a total of $6,734,782 in 1995 lobbying lawmakers in Sacramento. This amount dwarfs the spending by well-known special interest groups such as the dairy lobby and the horseracing lobby, and it does not even include direct contributions to candidates for office. Many of these entities are school districts or county offices of education that are spending *our tax money,* levied locally, to lobby at the state level for *more* taxes and spending for government-run schools. Following are the top ten spenders and the amounts they spent:

1.	California Teachers Association (NEA affiliate)	$1,103,344
2.	California School Boards Association	889,271
3.	California School Employees Association	749,523
4.	Association of California School Administrators	400,102
5.	Los Angeles Unified School District	385,119
6.	California Federation of Teachers (AFT affiliate)	226,587
7.	Los Angeles County Office of Education	153,802
8.	San Diego Unified School District	132,925
9.	California County Superintendents Association	131,583
10.	Alhambra School District	129,139
	TOTAL	$4,301,395

Source: "Lobbying Expenditures and the Top 100 Lobbying Firms, 1996" (Sacramento, CA: Office of the Secretary of State of California, June 1996).

Until recently, this largesse benefited mainly the Democratic party, but in 1996 the NEA changed its tactics and began donating to *all* incumbents who would support its agenda, regardless of party affiliation. At the Republican party convention in San Diego in August 1996, the CTA left a packet on the chair of each delegate, stating that since October 1994, more than $300,000 had been given to California GOP candidates, "and more will be given between now and election day." The union operatives distributing the packets made ominous references to the press about the "defunding" of public education—a curious point of view, considering the skyrocketing per student expenditures in public schools in the United States.

Sadly, almost all of this buying of political influence has been to the detriment of our children. In one of his more astonishing quotes, Albert Shanker said, *"When schoolchildren start paying union dues, that's when I'll start representing the interests of schoolchildren."* Mary Futrell, the NEA president from 1981 to 1989, summed up the dominant attitude of teachers union bosses in less pungent but equally clear terms: "Instruction and professional development have been on the back burner for us, compared with political action."

Both the NEA and the AFT have consistently opposed all reforms that could improve public education: student testing, teacher competency testing, merit pay, an end to the tenure system that makes public school teaching a job guaranteed for life—and, of course, school choice. Their opposition to reform was taken to an absurd new high (or low) in 1996, when the local NEA affiliate in Hartford, Connecticut filed a lawsuit against higher teacher standards, in which it claimed that ". . . no relation has ever been shown between teachers [qualifications] and student achievement"—a truly mind-boggling statement to put into writing in a public legal document.

The unions' opposition to school choice stops at their own door, of course, as documented in Chapter 7. Increasingly, union members send their own children to private schools, while loudly denouncing the efforts of others to obtain that right for everyone. In a 1994 TV debate in which George Will charged that big-city public school teachers send their own kids to private schools at a rate 50 percent higher than that of the general public, a flustered Keith Geiger, president of the NEA, blurted, "It's not 50 percent; it's 40 percent."

As mentioned in Chapter 9, through the 1988 movie *Stand and Deliver*, a dedicated Los Angeles math teacher named Jaime Escalante became a national hero for his brilliant work with barrio kids at Garfield High School. In 1991 he fled to Sacramento, writing to his union president, "If you look at what is going on in this school in the name of the union, I think you . . . would be appalled." In February 1996, he commented to a *U.S. News & World Report* journalist, "I thought the union was going to focus on how to improve our skills. But they're more interested in politics than kids."

Ideally, the teachers unions could again become what they once were: professional associations dedicated to improving the standards of the teaching profession. But this could occur only in an educational system in which the conditions of their employment are determined by negotiation with the families they serve, not with politicians they have bought and now own. Teachers will once again have the professional respect and status they deserve when they work in a system in which families have freely chosen their schools because they value the teachers. With parents and teachers once again working *together*, rather than as adversaries, they could achieve a common goal: the education and well-being of our children.

The NEA in Its Own Words

Within ten years, I think this organization will control the qualifications for entrance into the profession, and for the privilege of remaining in the profession.
— George Fischer, past president, NEA
NEA Convention, 1970

We are the biggest potential striking force in this country, and we are determined to control the direction of education.
— Catherine Barrett, past president, NEA
Washington Star News, 1972

We want a legislative program led by leaders and staff with sufficient clout that they may roam the halls of Congress and collect votes to reorder the priorities of the United States of America.
— Terry Herndon, former executive director, NEA
NEA Convention, 1978

The major purpose of our association is not the education of children; it is or ought to be the extension and/or preservation of our members' rights. We earnestly care about the kids learning, but that is secondary to the other goals.
— *NEA Oregon UniServ Bulletin,* October 1981

[Our] plan calls for . . . autonomous state agencies, governed by teachers and other professional educators, with the power to approve teacher preparation programs and certify practitioners.

— NEA Action Plan
NEA Today, November 1982

In the 1960s we took a rather quiet, genteel professional association of educators, and we reinvented it as an assertive—and, when necessary, militant—labor union.

— Robert Chase, president, NEA
The Washington Times, February 6, 1997

The following quotes were all taken from the 1992–93 Resolutions of the NEA, published in *NEA Today,* September 1992.

The National Education Association believes that competency testing must not be used as a condition of employment, license retention, evaluation, placement, ranking, or promotion of licensed teachers. The Association also opposes the use of pupil progress, standardized achievement tests, or student assessment tests for purposes of teacher evaluation.

The Association urges the elimination of state statutes/regulations that require teachers to renew their licenses. Where such renewal continues to be required, standardized literacy and basic skills tests to determine competency should not be used.

The Association believes that performance pay schedules, such as merit pay, are inappropriate.

The Association believes that there should be no single or statewide accountability system. . . . The Association believes that specific behavioral objectives should not be used as course objectives or as a basis for determining accountability.

The National Education Association believes that any mandated standards for educational programs should set only broad, general guidelines and should not be based on student achievement.

Chapter 12

ZIP Code Segregation in the Public Schools

Carlos A. Bonilla

The perception throughout the country of continually declining standards in the public school system, lower SAT scores, high dropout rates, gangs, drugs, and violence provides an impetus for developers and real estate agents to market their properties on the basis of their proximity to "good, clean, safe public schools." Just glance at some recent newspaper articles and real estate advertisements:

➤ "Realtors Take Tour to Sell Home Buyers on Schools," *The San Diego Union Tribune,* June 9, 1996.

➤ "High-Ranking Schools Bag Big-Bucks Housing," *San Francisco Examiner,* July 14, 1996.

➤ "A Deciding Factor: Education—If You Want a House Near a Good School . . . [it] can be Expensive," *Sacramento Bee,* May 1, 1994.

➤ "Smart Moves: Many Families Are Willing to Pull Up Roots to Find 'Good Schools,'" *Los Angeles Times,* February 4, 1996.

➤ "Location, Location, Location: Better Schools Mean Higher Property Values," *USA Today,* May 15, 1996.

This chapter is adapted from an editorial by Carlos A. Bonilla in the *Stockton Record,* February 23, 1992. The author gratefully acknowledges the assistance of Gay Hardwick in preparing this revision.

Obviously, it pays to be wealthy; being poor can be harmful to one's educational health. In California, Latino and African-American parents filed a lawsuit in 1992 against the Los Angeles Unified School District in an attempt to correct teaching imbalances among the district's 640 campuses. The suit addressed the tendency for higher-paid veteran teachers to go to suburban campuses, forcing inner-city schools to rely on lower-paid, novice instructors. It led to what is known as the *Rodriguez* consent decree—meaning that the plaintiffs won their case.

In California as well as throughout the United States, however, there is still a major gap in public education. It is racially and economically based, and it is becoming ever wider. It is a tragedy that, despite the valiant battles for racial equality fought by Dr. Martin Luther King, Jr., and many others, this is still a fact of life in America as we approach the twenty-first century.

The consequences of this education gap are stark. The reading and writing skills of the average black or Hispanic twelfth-grader in public schools are far below those of the average white student. While over two-thirds of all white students take geometry, fewer than 50 percent of blacks do. While 56 percent of whites take the two-year sequence of algebra, only 40 percent of black students do. In science, minority students also trail white students, as indicated by the results of tests administered by the Educational Testing Service; these results have not changed significantly since 1976, when ethnicity data were instituted.

Here are some of the reasons for the gap, or should we say, the segregation of children's education according to where they live—what I call *ZIP code segregation:*

➤   Teachers and administrators in inner-city public schools and schools in poverty-ridden areas have low expectations and standards for students, and place them on low-achievement tracks.

➤   Qualified teachers in these schools are siphoned off to the better schools in more affluent areas; the critical shortage of competent instructors creates an educational vacuum.

The forcible assignment of public school students to particular schools based on geographic residence virtually guarantees school segregation, in terms of both race and economic class. The privilege of living in an exclusive school district can be extraordinarily expensive. In this example from a Northern California real estate development, the lowest-priced home costs $734,000.

➤ These schools generally lack science labs, computers, and other equipment necessary to impart the required knowledge.

➤ When computers and other modern technologies are available in these schools, they are used for drilling in the basics or for rote learning, rather than for training in advanced skills, as they are in schools in the more affluent areas.

All over the United States, the public education albatross segregates students according to the new math of rich and poor. In many states (although less so in California, because of the 1978 *Serrano* decision), there is a direct correlation between a community's wealth and its expenditure for public education. It stands to reason that a public school system that forces students into a particular school based on geographic residence, no matter how bad that school is, will result in children from ethnic ghettos being segregated in inferior schools.

This inequity has led to landmark decisions by the courts in response to lawsuits seeking more equity in the financing of public schools. In New Jersey's 1990 *Abbott* v. *Burke* supreme court decision, the court determined that the fifty-four richest school districts were spending 40 percent more, on average, than the twenty-eight poorest school districts. This resulted in such inequities as a rich school district in Princeton having one computer for every eight children, while a poor district in Camden had only one computer for every fifty-eight children. Thus, the public schools were spending the least money on the children who most needed help to avoid a life of welfare or crime at enormous cost to the taxpayers. The court ordered the spending equalized— an order it had to reissue in 1994 owing to noncompliance.

Many urban areas of the United States have resorted to forced busing to remedy these inequities, but that is not the answer. Forced busing is so disruptive to the social fabric that many higher-income families leave the school district entirely to avoid it. They either move to the suburbs or put their children in private schools—either way resulting in more public school racial segregation than ever. Forced busing results in some families' paying taxes and voting in one school district while sending their children to school in another district, making a mockery of the most basic principles of representative democracy. The ultimate irony is that forced busing is highly unpopular with the very people it claims to help: low-income and minority families.

By almost any standard, our nation's private schools are better racially integrated than our highly segregated public schools, even though private school families almost invariably have to pay for the tuition from their own pockets. Imagine how much improvement in racial integration there would be if each family could freely choose the education of its children. Such diverse experiences as the Polly Williams voucher program in Milwaukee and California's charter schools have shown that racial harmony and voluntary integration result from the only hope we have for an end to the pernicious racial segregation in our public schools: school choice that includes independent schools.

Under a voucher system, all families receive substantially the same tax money for schooling, unlike the more-money-for-the-rich public schools in New Jersey. With freedom of choice, families could be counted on to enroll their children in schools that demanded high performance from *all* children, and to avoid schools that made all kinds of excuses as to why inner-city children can't learn. Given the kind of stable communities that result from school choice, teachers would have an incentive to make a commitment to a school in which they could take pride and a sense of accomplishment, rather than fleeing dysfunctional inner-city public schools at the first opportunity.

School choice represents our best hope for a return to America as the land of opportunity, where ambition and hard work count for more than what side of the tracks you were born on.

Adelante.

Chapter 13

Rx for the Hispanic Dropout Crisis

Carlos A. Bonilla

We have a major social crisis on our hands—a sort of national epidemic caused by the severe undereducation of a particular ethnic group: Hispanics.[1] In singling out Hispanics, I do not intend to minimize the educational problems of other ethnic groups, but the Latino community is the one I know best, and its problems are crucial for another, central reason: it is now clear that, in the long run, Hispanics will be by far the largest ethnic minority group, not just in California, but in the United States as a whole.

The nature of the epidemic can be summarized as follows:

Patient:	Hispanic youth
Symptoms:	Failure to thrive
Diagnosis:	Chronic educational malnutrition
Condition:	Critical

But all is not lost. As is true in complicated medical cases, the best approach to making the correct diagnosis, finding solutions, and suggesting potential treatment regimes is to discuss the patient's history and reasons for his or her condition in a detailed and honest manner. So let us do that, and perhaps *this* critical patient—Latino youth—will make a miraculous recovery. Miracles *can* be made to happen, as Part II of this book amply illustrates.

---

[1] Throughout this work, the terms Hispanic and Latino are used interchangeably. Hispanics, an ethnic group, can be of any race and do not necessarily have their origins in Latin America.

The number of Hispanics entering the U.S. population annually now exceeds that of non-Hispanic whites. This turning point in the history of U.S. demographics occurred during fiscal year 1993–94, when, according to the latest census figures, the Hispanic population increased by 902,000 while the non-Hispanic white population increased by 883,000. This pattern was repeated during fiscal year 1994–95 and is expected to continue well into the next century, when, for the first time, non-Hispanic whites will make up less than 50 percent of the nation's population (in mid-1996 they stood at 72 percent).

In other words, sometime during the first half of the twenty-first century, the United States will become a "minority-majority" country. California, however, is expected to reach minority-majority status during the next four to seven years.

What are some of the potential impacts of this unprecedented shift in U.S. demographics? Let us look at the estimated U.S. population figures for 1996:

Non-Hispanic Whites	191,718,000
Blacks	33,618,000
Hispanics	27,937,000
Asian/Pacific Islanders	9,638,000
Native Americans	2,275,000
TOTAL	265,186,000

Now consider the following scenario:

➤ The non-Hispanic white population is entering the aging/senior ranks at a far greater rate than other ethnic groups.

➤ Consequently, the work force is becoming increasingly made up of minorities.

➤ Not far in the future, seniors will become significantly dependent on the Social Security taxes paid by young minorities in the labor market.

➤ Latinos are highly overrepresented in jobs that are becoming obsolete because of rapid advances in technology.

➤ Failure to address the undereducation of Latino youth will therefore result in staggering economic and social problems.

The children of our fast-growing Latino population now form the second-largest ethnic group of youngsters in the United States. They are growing in numbers, but they are *not* thriving. They face educational, health, and poverty woes that, in the present political and social climate, are very difficult to overcome. And these problems are worsening all the time, in part because of the extraordinarily high Hispanic dropout rate from our public schools.

The numbers and growth rates of the three largest categories of American children are as follows:

Children's Population (millions)

	1990	1996	Growth Rate
Non-Hispanic Whites	49.2	50.8	3.3%
Hispanics	9.8	12.0	22.4%
Non-Hispanic Blacks	10.4	11.4	9.6%

According to U.S. Department of Education figures, the high school dropout rate among Hispanics in the age group 16–24 is 29.4 percent—more than twice as high as that of blacks and almost four times as high as that of whites. *The undereducation of Latino youth represented by this appalling statistic can only be viewed as a national crisis.* Even for Latino students who remain in school, however, achievement levels continue to be well below national averages, as shown in the following table:

Average SAT Scores (1993–94)

	Verbal	Mathematical
All Students	423	479
Whites	443	495
Blacks	352	388
Mexican-Americans	372	427
Puerto Ricans	367	411
Asian-Americans	416	535
Native Americans	396	441

Other factors—gang affiliations, drug use, high teen pregnancy rates, poor health, and fear of violence in the schools, among others—play key roles in the poor educational attainment of Latino youth. These fall outside the scope of this discussion, but all are problems that tend to be alleviated when children are allowed to attend schools of choice.

The abandonment of Hispanic youth by the public school monopoly is beyond dispute and is perhaps best illustrated by the dropout statistic cited above. The highest dropout rates of all, not surprisingly, are among children born outside the United States, who often have poor English skills: *43 percent* of these non-native children fail to finish high school. What is truly shocking, however, is that second-generation Hispanics have a higher dropout rate than first-generation: 23.7 percent versus 17.3 percent. Thus, American-born Hispanics who have been here *longer* are doing *worse* than those who are the children of Hispanics born outside the United States.

What this tells us is that a one-size-fits-all public school monopoly lumping all Hispanics into one category is failing this crucial ethnic group. Hispanics can be separated into at least five well-differentiated groups, which range from the poor migrant worker family to the third- or fourth-generation Latino-American families of moderate or even great wealth. A faceless and unresponsive bureaucracy cannot make subtle distinctions among different categories of Hispanics with widely varying cultural as well as economic backgrounds. What the Latino community desperately needs is the freedom and dignity to choose for its own children the most appropriate education.

The parents of Latino children must be made to feel welcome and valued in the public school system. Their opinions must be heard and taken seriously. They should be empowered to choose their own schools and to have the leverage of being able to vote with their feet if they are not listened to and treated with dignity and respect. Their continued exclusion from the system will only exacerbate the decline of K–12 education.

No group has been harmed more by the public school monopoly than the Latino community, and no group would benefit more from school choice. It is no surprise, therefore, that opinion polls have shown Hispanics to be the strongest supporters of vouchers. In a 1991 Gallup poll, the general public supported school choice by 50 percent, but blacks supported it by 57 percent, and a whopping 84 percent of Hispanics supported it. Our Latino community desperately needs better schools, and we need to be able to choose them for ourselves if we are to advance our pursuit of the American dream.

Gracias. Muchisimas gracias. Bueno, pues aqui vamos!

Chapter 14

Are There *Any* Valid Arguments Against School Choice?

Many of the most common arguments against school choice are dealt with elsewhere in this book. The constitutionality of school choice is addressed in "Safe Sex, Safe Religion" (Chapter 29). The argument that it is the government's duty to impose common values on children through compulsory government schooling is dealt with in "Freedom of Schooling as a Human Right" (Chapter 30). The claim that school choice will result in worsening racial segregation is debunked both in the chapter on charter schools, "A School for the Next Century" (Chapter 3), and in "ZIP Code Segregation in the Public Schools" (Chapter 12). The former cites the Little Hoover Commission's report that California's charter schools are *at least* as well integrated as its public schools. And certainly no one who has read this far in this book could possibly believe the claim that school choice is somehow untried or unproved.

What follows, therefore, are some of the other common objections to school choice that need to be addressed—and put to rest.

1. We can't afford school choice. Millions of private school children will pour into the system, bankrupting us.

The exact opposite is true. Because private schools cost so much less (about half, on average) than public schools, every voucher-based school choice system that has ever been proposed or implemented in the United States has offered a smaller voucher than the per student cost in public schools. Thus, every time a student leaves a public school for a private school, there is a *saving* to the taxpayers.

But there *is* a complicating factor: we have to provide vouchers for students *already* in private schools. This could initially create a serious funding deficit—but only if the private school students became eligible for vouchers *immediately*, as was true of the ill-fated Amendment 7 on the Colorado ballot in November 1992.

To avoid that problem, Proposition 174 on the California ballot in November 1993 stipulated that all private school students (about 10 percent of the total school enrollment) would be ineligible for vouchers for the first two years of the program. This would have allowed a sufficient surplus of funds to build up from the transfer of students from public to private schools during those two years to cover the cost of the vouchers for all previously enrolled private school students when they *did* become eligible in the third year of the program.

The opposition to Prop. 174, however, saturated the television and radio airwaves with the claim that hundreds of thousands of private school children would be *immediately* eligible for vouchers, at a cost of billions of dollars to the taxpayers. Millions of dollars in CTA money were spent in promoting this lie. Although it was not allowed in the voter's handbook, because it *was* a lie, it did its job effectively. The fact that every major taxpayer group in the state endorsed Prop. 174 because of the billions of dollars it would have saved the taxpayers over the long run did not become widely known.

Two of the three publicly funded voucher programs in the United States that include private schools—the Milwaukee and Cleveland programs—are for low-income families only, as are all of the twenty-eight privately funded voucher programs. Since so few low-income families can now afford private schools, the savings to the taxpayers with this type of program are even more dramatic, proportionally, than with a universal voucher.

In truth, we can't afford *not* to have a voucher system. Throughout the nation, projected increases in school enrollment will rapidly outstrip our ability to build new schools during the next decade unless we adopt a system of school choice that can provide superior education at lower cost.

2. Private schools would provide inferior education under a voucher system, because they employ noncredentialed teachers.

Under school choice, any private school could insist on hiring only credentialed teachers and could use this as a selling point if it could convince parents that this was important. There are strong reasons, however, for *not* making this a requirement of any choice program. California's current private schools, almost none of which require teacher credentialing, are producing *improving* SAT scores at the same time its public schools are producing *declining* SAT scores. Why should we copy a system that's failing?

A 1989 study by the RAND Corporation found a positive correlation between the amount of course-work preparation by science and mathematics teachers and student learning in those fields. This is hardly surprising, and it's probably true in all other fields as well. By contrast, however, there is no known correlation—except perhaps a *negative* one—between teacher credentialing and student achievement. As counterintuitive as this seems, there are valid reasons for it—not the least of which are the incredibly low standards of teacher proficiency required in the credentialing process, as exemplified by California's notorious CBEST examination (see the sidebar in Chapter 8).

It is widely acknowledged that a large majority of graduates of teacher training programs are coming from the bottom third of their college classes. Almost inevitably, then, insisting on credentialed teachers will generally result in *poorer,* not better, teachers. As the late Albert Shanker, president of the American Federation of Teachers, said, "Most of America's college graduates who are going into public school teaching wouldn't be able to get into college in any other country." And his well-known remark about the dumbing down of our public school teachers in the 1990s is quoted in Chapter 8.

In an excellent new report, "California Index of Leading Education Indicators," Lance Izumi of the Pacific Research Institute reveals that the percentage of American mathematics teachers who actually have a degree in mathematics is shockingly low.[1] (In the state ranking, California comes in dead last, at 39 percent.) Thorough knowledge of one's subject has taken a backseat to

---

[1] Lance Takeo Izumi, "California Index of Leading Educational Indicators" (San Francisco: Pacific Research Institute, 1997).

credentialing, which does not seem to require it. For the final word on teacher credentialing, see Dr. Anyim Palmer's comment on this subject in Chapter 20.

3. School choice will result in cult schools affiliated with the likes of Jim Jones and his People's Temple.

There are currently millions of children enrolled in private schools throughout the United States, yet the opponents of school choice have *never* been able to point to a single cult school anywhere, because the existence of such schools is prohibited by the education codes of all fifty states. And *every* proposal for school choice in the United States has explicitly excluded schools that teach racial, ethnic, or religious hatred.

The oft-cited People's Temple experience is especially ironic: before moving to Guyana, the "Reverend" Jim Jones's cult was instrumental in electing two members of San Francisco's Board of Education. And prior to the cult's mass suicide, they gunned down U.S. Representative Leo Ryan, who had volunteered to lead California's 1978 school choice effort and who was in Guyana to investigate the cult's activities.

4. If private schools go bankrupt, students will be left stranded in mid-term.

To minimize the chances of fiscal irresponsibility or mismanagement, virtually every school choice proposal has mandated that the private schools be paid on a month-by-month basis. This will not only ensure a stable cash flow but will also give parents the leverage they need to change to a different school if they are dissatisfied.

The question, as well, presupposes that it is only private schools that go bankrupt, which is far from the case. The Washington, DC schools have been effectively bankrupt for years, and will probably be taken over this year by the federal government. Despite a budget that would rank the District of Columbia fifth in the nation in per student spending if it were a state, the schools there have been so badly mismanaged that in many years they have been unable to open on time because of neglected building maintenance. Recently the school district officials have been unable even to give an accurate count of the number of students enrolled!

In California, the Compton and Richmond school districts *are* bankrupt. Embarrassment over the Richmond district's total disarray despite massive state aid may be one reason why it is fraudulently reporting its per student expenditures as being *less* than California's Average Daily Attendance subsidy. This claim is all the more outrageous when one recalls that the district receives federal, county, and local funding in addition to state funding.

5. What if everyone wants to go to the same school of choice?

They can't, of course. But we now have abundant experience with school choice around the world; in European countries allowing school choice that includes private schools at the elementary and secondary levels—which is to say, *all* Western European countries—the problem is not a shortage of schools of choice, but rather excess capacity.[2]

In a free market system, when an enterprise succeeds, it expands and establishes new branches, and its competitors copy it and try to improve on it. By contrast, the American public school monopoly has steadfastly refused to offer the public the kinds of schools that have succeeded. In San Francisco, for example, Lowell High School offers a rigorous science curriculum and maintains demanding standards. Yet, despite the excellent reputation of this school and the long waiting list of parents eager to enroll their children there, the public school establishment has refused to create other schools like Lowell, and it restricts entry to that exclusive high school to the chosen few. One can only ask: *Why?*

6. What if the public schools are unable to compete with the new schools of choice, and the public school system is destroyed?

What a revealing question! If it is really true that the public schools are unable to compete, even with much more money per student than what a voucher program would offer private schools, even with their real estate already largely paid for, and even with a public already familiar with their product,

---

[2] Paradoxically, and again in striking contrast with the United States, there are virtually no private colleges or universities in Europe. Although there is great freedom of choice within the system of *public* colleges and universities, the lack of competition from the private sector seems detrimental: the American system of higher education is widely acknowledged to be superior. Thus it appears that the broadest-based freedom of choice and the best results go hand-in-hand.

then we are truly in desperate straits. It is amazing that the public school monopoly would offer such an argument—that their service is so inferior that they will be unable to compete and unable to improve even when faced with competition and a loss of their students.

In fact, *every* system of school choice has resulted in higher public school standards and, ultimately, a stabilizing in the relative market share between public and private schools. In the United States, for example, the school choice that we have in higher education through the GI Bill, Pell Grants, and government-guaranteed student loans has meant *higher* quality through competition and freedom of choice among all public universities and within multicampus public universities such as the University of California. Nationwide, there has actually been an *increase* in the percentage of students attending public vs. private universities in the United States over the last fifty years.

Perhaps the most relevant example to the United States is the establishment of voucher systems in all the states of Australia, starting in the 1960s, and in Canada, primarily in British Columbia, starting in 1977. The experience of both of these countries, which are closer to the United States culturally and economically than any others, was that school choice initially prompted a flight of students to private schools, followed by an upgrading of standards by the public schools and an eventual stabilization in market share.

Finally, of course this argument doesn't even apply to the many school choice programs throughout the United States for disadvantaged students only. Had Governor Pete Wilson's Opportunity Scholarships bill passed in California in 1996, only students attending the lowest-performing 5 percent of schools would have been eligible for the scholarships. Relieving the public schools of this burden and leaving them with the 95 percent of better-performing students scarcely bears the seeds of destroying the public school system.

7. The United States Constitution guarantees a public school education to every child.

No, it does not. Although this canard is often repeated by public school officials debating school choice, the United States Constitution is, in fact, silent on the issue of education. The constitution was ratified in 1788, but the first state-supported school in America—a normal school in Lexington, Massachusetts—was not founded until fifty-one years later, in 1839, by Horace Mann. Nor was the concept a home-grown idea: the American public schools that soon followed were modeled after the Prussian compulsory government schools of that era.

8. Voucher systems such as the GI Bill, Pell Grants, and Cal-Grants may be suitable for higher education, but not for the elementary and secondary levels, which are fundamentally different.

This is a curious argument indeed, considering that a federally mandated voucher system for *preschoolers* is in place for all fifty states, the District of Columbia, all U.S. territories and possessions, and all Indian tribes. The program, called the Child Care and Development Block Grant (CCDBG), was enacted by Congress in 1990; it took effect on a voluntary basis in 1991 and became mandatory on October 1, 1992.

The CCDBG program is a means-tested voucher system for low-income families, covering preschool *and* after-school daycare for children through age twelve (regardless of grade level). Parents may use the vouchers at any authorized preschool or daycare facility of their choice, including religious providers. The latter are free to redeem vouchers because the money is under the direct control of the parents and not the state. (The program also provides for direct contracts between the state and authorized facilities; religious providers are *not* eligible for these contracts. The state of California is issuing vouchers, but no contracts.)

Initial funding for the CCDBG was $1 billion per year (California received $100.6 million in FY 1992–93). In August 1996, however, the program's funding was tripled to $2.967 billion per year, with strong bipartisan support. California's share of this amount for FY 1996–97 is $309.6 million, and it is estimated that this amount is funding about 80,000 vouchers. The actual amount of the vouchers is set by each state on a sliding scale, depending on the family's need, and some copayments are required.[3]

---

[3] Readers who wish more information on this ground-breaking voucher program should contact Dr. William J. Tobin, of William J. Tobin & Associates, 3612 Bent Branch Court, Falls Church, VA 22041. He can be reached at (703) 941–4329.

The program is apparently held in high regard by Congress, and, significantly, has not inspired a single legal challenge anywhere. There have been no reports of state governments imposing new or tougher regulations on pre-schools or daycare centers as a result of the program, nor has there been a single report of voucher-redeeming facilities being run by witches or Nazis (favorite speculations by hysterical opponents of school choice). By all these measures, at least, the program must be judged a success.

In conclusion, we offer a question of our own, to all opponents of vouchers or any other mechanism for granting freedom of schooling:

Considering that we in America have nearly unlimited freedom of choice in virtually every aspect of our lives, *why is it* that educational freedom is OK for preschoolers, daycare children, college students, graduate students, and trade and professional school students, but *not* for K–12 students?

Chapter 15

In the Beginning

Alan Bonsteel

The school choice effort entered my life like a bolt of lightning. One day in 1979, I came upon a story in the *San Francisco Chronicle* about two law professors in Berkeley, John Coons and Stephen Sugarman, who were running a citizens initiative that would allow California families to choose their own schools. This was the first serious political effort for school choice in the nation. I knew instantly that it was something I wanted to help with, and for the rest of that year I was a spear carrier, standing on street corners asking for signatures.

My own California high school in San Jose had been a prison for me. I chafed at being trapped in a school in which the principal couldn't write a sentence across the blackboard without making glaring errors in spelling and grammar, and I rebelled against the shallow and materialistic values we were taught. Nothing will ever turn back the clock and give me the positive school experience I wish I'd had, but I want to light a candle for the children of today, to make sure that someday no child will be held captive in a school that is indifferent to his needs and desires. And so, perhaps that bolt of lightning in 1979, that sense that this work was *meant* for me, wasn't just out of the blue.

In 1979 we attempted to qualify for the 1980 ballot, but failed. In early 1980, Coons and Sugarman announced that they were postponing any further efforts. They had combat fatigue, but I was fresh and had barely gotten warmed up. Although I had never met them, I called them on the phone and pleaded with them to continue. They were noncommittal, but agreed to meet me at UC Berkeley's Faculty Club.

The 1978–1979 effort, although it had generated enormous publicity and put educational choice on the map, both in California and nationwide, had nevertheless been a trial in other ways. Coons had persuaded U.S. Representative Leo Ryan to lead the effort; only months later, in late 1978, Ryan was murdered in Guyana during the mass suicide of the People's Temple cult while he was investigating that group. Coons and Sugarman then engaged a political consultant to handle the campaign. When the consultant discovered that there were no special interest groups that could donate large amounts of money to the campaign, he lost interest himself, and it was discovered only too late that he was rumored to have underworld connections.

What was lifting the spirits of Coons and Sugarman by the time I met them at the Faculty Club was the response of many of the grassroots campaign workers, who, like myself, were phoning to tell them that school reform was too important to drop, and offering their support for another try. It was hard to think of anyone more qualified for the job of reforming our schools than Coons and Sugarman. In 1970 they had written, with William Clune, the classic book *Private Wealth and Public Education*. In 1971, and again in 1978, they had argued and won the *Serrano* case in the California Supreme Court. That decision established the duty of the state to be "fiscally neutral" in its financing of public schools. The spirit of the *Serrano* decision was followed by many other state courts, establishing the constitutional right to be free of discrimination by wealth in government schools. In 1978 Coons and Sugarman took the principle one step further, arguing, in the book *Education by Choice: The Case for Family Control,* that in a society in which the rich have always been able to choose schools for their children, the poor should also have that ability.

For my part, I had made a stake in California real estate during the years of double-digit inflation and could make a good living on only about thirty hours of work per week, giving me the time to try to put together a campaign. Besides, I had an idea: in 1976, third-party presidential candidate John Anderson had taken out full-page newspaper ads asking people to donate to his campaign; with dissatisfaction with Carter and Ford running high, it had worked. I proposed that we take out an ad in *Time* magazine in California only, asking people to help us, and I offered to lend the campaign the $5,000 needed for this.

The first-ever political ad for school choice in the United States. It ran in Time *magazine on June 16, 1980. By sheer coincidence, the cover story for that issue was entitled, "Help! Teacher Can't Teach!"*

The ad, as it turned out, didn't bring in enough contributions to pay for itself, and I've since learned that the John Anderson ad was a phenomenon that almost no other political effort has ever duplicated. But our ad, seen in the June 16, 1980 issue by all of *Time* magazine's California readers, was the shot heard 'round the world that jump-started a new effort. By sheer dumb luck, it appeared in an issue with the cover story, "Help! Teacher Can't Teach!" about incompetent public school teachers. The combination of the cover story and our hard-hitting ad created quite a stir.

We opened an office on Mission Street in San Francisco, almost next door to the *Chronicle* building. We organized the names of all the people who had helped us in 1978–1979 into a mailing list and sent them a newsletter every three months, along with a request for donations, which would be our main source of funds for the next two years. Other important financial contributors were Joe Alibrandi, the CEO of Whittaker Corporation, and Don Sebastiani of the vintner family. Our key people began to meet on an almost monthly basis. One of the most important activists was Dennis Revell, husband of Maureen Reagan, Ronald Reagan's daughter—although this connection unfortunately never translated into direct help from the president.

Also in 1980, Coons appeared on Dr. Milton Friedman's *Free to Choose* television series in the segment on school choice, along with Albert Shanker, president of the American Federation of Teachers. Although for many years, Coons and Friedman have held different points of view about the best approach to school choice, that particular debate ended with the two of them ganging up on Shanker. Interestingly, Shanker (who passed away as this book was being edited) was edging closer in recent years to advocating a more market-based public school system, likening the current American public school system to a "Soviet command-based economy." He even toyed with the idea of a private school voucher for children who are failing in public schools. Many of the teachers-union bosses are purely money- and power-motivated, but Shanker was considered a worthy opponent by almost all in the educational choice movement. His honesty and intellectual vitality on that side of the debate will be missed.

At the same time that we were promoting a school voucher effort for the 1982 ballot, the Libertarian party proposed a school tax credit called the ETC, for Educational Tax Credit. It didn't take a rocket scientist to see that if the two groups could unify their efforts on a common proposal, we would maximize our chances of qualifying for the ballot. In 1981 a negotiation toward that end was sponsored by Dr. Frank Fortcamp, representing the Koch family of Kansas, and held in the Clift Hotel in San Francisco.

The problem with tax credits is that poor families don't pay enough in taxes—especially state taxes, over which a state initiative would have control—for a tax credit to be of any use. Even middle-income taxpayers pay less in state taxes than the average private school tuition. State tax credits also suffer from a problem Coons and Sugarman have dubbed "revenue sharing in reverse." Since state taxes are a deduction from federal taxes, a state educational tax credit *increases* federal taxes. The Libertarians had tried to get around the problem of people too poor to pay state taxes by allowing rich taxpayers with no children in school to give away their educational tax credits. This largesse, however, would have come at the price of increasing the federal taxes of the persons giving away the tax credits.

It is possible to design a refundable tax credit—meaning one available even for those who pay little or no state taxes—that would meet some of these objections. Such an approach would not solve the "revenue sharing in reverse" problem, but that may be a small price to pay for the protection a tax credit gives to private schools from unwarranted government interference.

The bottom line for us was that we were committed to a proposal that would give the poor—the group most in need of educational choice—if not equal access, then at least fair access to schools of choice. Unfortunately, the two groups were unable to agree on a compromise measure, and, as it turned out, neither one qualified for the ballot. The Libertarians then proceeded to qualify in 1984 for the ballot in Washington, DC, where the smaller population requires far fewer signatures. The educational tax credit proposal was perceived as helping the rich at the expense of the poor, however, and it went down by a 7-to-1 margin.

Our main strategy in trying to qualify for the 1982 ballot was to get the Catholic parochial schools to help us financially and with volunteers, and to assemble a broad enough coalition that the issue wouldn't be seen as a

"Catholic" one. At that time, Catholic schools enrolled about 70 percent of all of California's private school students (it is now about 50 percent), and they were the only private school group that was really a system that could work in a well-coordinated way. They were therefore essential to a strategy based on the private schools' putting us on the ballot, but they couldn't go it alone. We were able to assemble some broad-based support from many of the other private schools, most notably the Lutheran, Seventh-Day Adventist, Baptist, and nondenominational Christian schools. Armed with this support, in 1981 Cardinal Timothy Manning of Los Angeles asked the other bishops of California to agree to help us financially and with volunteers.[1]

The twelve bishops of California met late that year to discuss Cardinal Manning's proposal, which we believed would succeed. To our dismay, however, the proposal was not approved, a great setback that we believe was caused by the vocal opposition of a single bishop. Without the Catholics, the remainder of our coalition was too small to have any realistic chance of putting us on the ballot. We abandoned our effort to qualify for 1982 and began to think about 1984.

It's frustrating, even now, to realize how close we came that far back to putting school choice on the ballot in California. We probably wouldn't have won the election, but by now there would have been several more efforts in California, rather than the single effort of Proposition 174 in 1993, and we might even have succeeded in passing a school choice proposal.

Times have changed since 1981. Then, the Catholic church could have given us enormous assistance in qualifying for the ballot and in the campaign itself. Now, I doubt that they could give us anywhere near the same help, because of the decline in their financial resources. And, both then and now, no school choice effort can afford to be seen as "just" a Catholic effort and have any hope of success.

On the other hand, more than half of all the private school students in California are attending Catholic schools, and it is almost unimaginable that

[1] For the information of those readers who, like myself, are not Catholic, a cardinal is the leader of one of the largest dioceses and has the right to vote for a new Pope. A cardinal, however, does not direct the work of other bishops, and any cooperative efforts are a matter of consensus.

a school choice effort could win without their support. One of the most serious mistakes of the Prop. 174 effort, discussed in detail in Chapter 25, was to ignore the counsel of the Catholic bishops and their representatives, and leave them no choice but to decline to endorse the initiative.

With the demise of the 1980–1981 effort, I decided to take an extended vacation at the end of 1981, planning to come back refreshed and ready for a try at the 1984 ballot. I flew to Nepal for two months of trekking in the Himalayas, and perhaps it's just as well that I was so isolated. I returned to the shock of discovering that the double-digit interest rates of the early 1980s had caused the real estate market to collapse while I was gone. I had no choice but to put my house and apartment buildings up for sale at rock-bottom prices, and the financial setback I suffered diminished my ability to participate in the school choice effort for years to come.

Despite its inauspicious beginning, the next year turned out to be quite fruitful in other ways—an idyll of low-budget travel interrupted only briefly by the "work" of visiting schools of choice in Australia and Israel. This trip was the first of seven I have made to visit systems of school choice overseas in a total of twelve countries. The time abroad also allowed me time to reflect on what to do next, and toward the end of the trip, I decided to enroll in medical school. I entered Dartmouth in New Hampshire in the fall of 1985.

During the years after our 1980–1981 effort, Coons and Sugarman initiated several more attempts, all of which fell short of the mark. In 1987, however, we again came tantalizingly close. Paul Gann, half of the Jarvis-Gann duo that had brought the tax-cutting Proposition 13 to the California voters, had built a citizens group that had qualified a whole series of initiatives for the California ballot—and most had won. He readily agreed that the next one would be a school choice initiative written by Coons and Sugarman. Gann's record in qualifying for the ballot was so sterling that I made arrangements to take a year off from medical school to assist the effort.

Tragically, however, Gann died of AIDS before the project could bear fruit. He contracted the illness from tainted blood during a transfusion for an operation. His loss was felt keenly not only by us, but by taxpayer activists nationwide.

Even though those years of effort never resulted in a qualification for the California ballot, they advanced the cause of educational choice in measurable ways. The publicity we generated in the 1978–1979 and 1980–1981 efforts nearly equaled that generated by Prop. 174, even though we never qualified for the ballot. And the *kind* of publicity showed the potential of a well-designed school choice initiative: we were all but endorsed by the *San Francisco Chronicle* and received extensive and favorable front-page coverage in the *Los Angeles Times*. The network of school choice advocates that resulted from our work ultimately made possible the qualification of Prop. 174, which in turn provided the impetus for the establishment of 100 charter schools in California. And we left for future efforts two important documents.

In the mid-1980s we were joined by Cliff Cobb, who went on to write the book *Responsive Schools, Renewed Communities,*[2] sponsored in part by a grant of money raised by two former members of our board of directors, Terry Taft and Richard Mushegain, and by Oakland Bishop John Cummins. Cobb's book has turned out to be a true classic in the field and has served as a reference for many school choice campaigns throughout the nation.

And in June 1980, Jack Coons published in *Newsweek* magazine's "My Turn" column the first argument for school choice ever seen in America's national news media. Reprinted here as Chapter 16, I still consider it the best thousand words ever published on school choice. Like Lincoln's Gettysburg Address, its very brevity gives it an impact far beyond what many books have had, and its words will live on in the battle for educational choice for years to come.

---

[2] Clifford W. Cobb, *Responsive Schools, Renewed Communities* (San Francisco: ICS Press, 1992).

Chapter 16

The Public School Monopoly

John E. Coons

The following essay was first published as a contribution to the "My Turn" column in *Newsweek* magazine, June 9, 1980.

Tax-supported schools call themselves public. The label is democratic, but the reality is not. To get the school you want for your child, you have to live in the right place in the right district. If the school is popular, getting a home there requires a deep pocket. You'd think such an elite system would be called private.

Meanwhile, schools called private take kids who live anywhere. Of course, they have to charge tuition to survive. Yet most make it on half the average cost of public schools and still give scholarships to many low-income pupils. Somehow they also keep their tuition down. In fact, they are a bargain. This helps explain why they often have so many low-income children; the Roman Catholic schools of California, for example, have a higher proportion of minority children statewide than do the public schools. Maybe private schools should be called public.

But private schools can subsidize only a fraction of those who apply. Hence, most families have no choice but to enroll their children in the schools to which they are assigned by an impersonal system of law. The system thus segregates children by income class—workers here, owners there. A Marxist would say, "It is no accident."

But it is. The system is not intentionally vicious. It is merely absurd.

Quality: Why worry? The kids all go to school. The problem is that choice affects quality in education as it does in art, sex, and anything else worthwhile. Children who attend public and private schools picked by their parents simply do better. They learn. They enjoy learning. They mature gracefully. They are more tolerant of individual differences. And this pattern holds irrespective of family income. Private schools in the slums turn out educated children.

At the same time, children from the same social class turn stupid and hostile in government schools enjoying twice the financial resources. They go there by compulsion. They tune out, drop out, are thrown out, or become professional truants. What they rarely do is flunk out. On the contrary, they graduate before it is discovered that they cannot read.

Is there something inherently wrong with government schools? Of course not. Some are splendid—especially those in neighborhoods inhabited by affluent families. But there is something seriously wanting in any school with a captive audience. Its managers have little reason to serve their clients; they have every reason to serve themselves.

"Public" schools are the quintessential self-serving monopoly. Unlike the local utility, they won't even disconnect and go away. You can rip out the phone, but you can't take your kid out of school. The school is not your servant but your master. It has no incentive to win you because it already has you.

1982, for example, would end teacher certification and tenure. Voucher schools would be free to set their own curricula, choose facilities, and govern themselves in a variety of ways. Parents would have a choice of style and content even in the public sector and would not be bound by district lines. Enrollment in the schools would be open and transportation provided for reasonable distances. Parents themselves could start public voucher schools by petition.

Regulators: The participating private schools under the California proposal would for the first time enjoy state constitutional protection against legislative regulation of hiring, cur-

---

To improve education, we should return to the small school operated by a faculty responsible to its clients.

The cure is obvious. The have-nots will be educated when they enjoy the liberty and responsibility that works for the wealthy. Call it "vouchers," call it what you will, but America desperately needs a system of family choice.

The machinery can be simple, flexible, and efficient. No existing institutions need be altered. A private school could forgo vouchers; a public school could be financed and administered as today. But families would now enjoy a choice among new public and private schools operating as individual institutions. These would be financed by state vouchers issued to the parents and cashed by their school. No pupils, no vouchers; no vouchers, no school. There would be a day of reckoning for educators.

Government voucher schools could be liberated from the maze of red tape. The California initiative planned for

ricula, and facilities. Their power to charge extra tuition would be limited, but they could seek support through voluntary giving. The participating private schools would continue as today, but they would have to provide fair disclosure of information—to ensure intelligent choice—and a neutral enrollment system. The only regulators would be the family and the school, not the state bureaucracy. Each child now would bring his own financial support in the form of a voucher.

The system would include private schools teaching religion; in education based upon choice, one would scarcely want to exclude them. Constitutional scholars give their blessing to the idea and predict its validation by the Supreme Court.

Choice would also give new hope for racial integration. Court orders generally stop at district lines; but voluntary transfers would cross those lines to reach schools public and private. They would open new space to the one form of integration that we know is stable—integration by choice. The polls show that the public supports voluntary integration as strongly as it rejects compulsory busing.

Perhaps the biggest winners in the new system would be teachers. Families favor schools that concentrate resources on teaching, not administration. Teachers would at last be in a solid economic position to start their own schools, and financial institutions would have reason to back them. We could do worse than return to the small school operated by a faculty responsible to its clients. Choice is the chief hope in the 1980s for a renaissance in education.

Part II

Does not love make us sensitive to things which are not noticed by others? Because he is in love with his world and not indifferent to it, a child's intelligence can see what is invisible to adults.

A child's love of his surroundings appears to adults as the natural joy and vitality of youth. But they do not recognize it as a spiritual energy, a moral beauty which accompanies creation.

— MARIA MONTESSORI

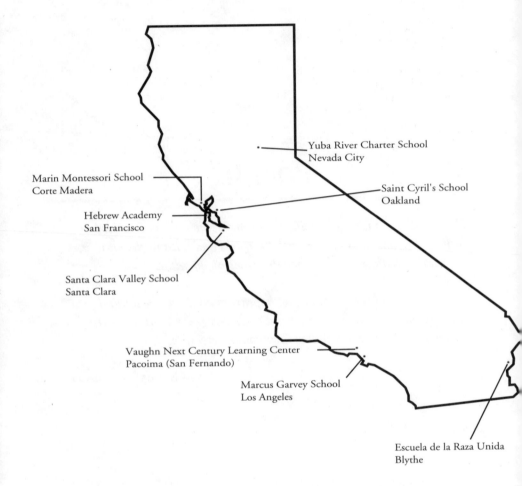

Yuba River Charter School
Nevada City

Marin Montessori School
Corte Madera

Saint Cyril's School
Oakland

Hebrew Academy
San Francisco

Santa Clara Valley School
Santa Clara

Vaughn Next Century Learning Center
Pacoima (San Fernando)

Marcus Garvey School
Los Angeles

Escuela de la Raza Unida
Blythe

Seven of the eight schools shown on this map of California are profiled in the following seven chapters (the Vaughn Next Century Learning Center was profiled in Chapter 3). Chapter 23 also profiles the Sudbury Valley School in Framingham, Massachusetts. It is noteworthy that, of these nine schools of choice (two of which are charter schools), eight spend less than California's per student cost for public schools, and all nine spend less than the national average for public schools.

Chapter 17

A Flower Blooms in the Desert

The hot sun of early summer beats mercilessly on the Mojave Desert town of Blythe, California. It is 117 degrees in the shade, but inside Carmela Garnica's storefront school, the students' spirits are high as the end of the school year nears. Almost all of them are the sons and daughters of Mexican immigrant farm workers, but they are talking excitedly in perfect English about their plans for the summer.

The school was born in 1972 as a result of profound dissatisfaction by the Hispanic community of Blythe with the public schools there. In the spring of that year, the principal of the local high school physically assaulted a female Hispanic honor roll student in front of multiple witnesses. After complaints to the school board were stonewalled, hundreds of Hispanic teenagers picketed the school. When the school board still didn't get it, parents met at the local United Farm Workers hall of Carmela's father, UFW organizer Alfredo Figueroa, and, with a *Si se Puede* ("Yes you Can") attitude, they founded what was first named the Freedom School.

For the last two months of the 1972 school year, the new school met in the open air at Todd Park, still used for their daily physical education activities. In the fall of 1972, the school reopened in the storefront that remains its home today under the new name of *Escuela de la Raza Unida* (School of the United People). Three hundred people came to the joyous opening ceremonies, marked by traditional dances and a banquet. Later, UFW leader César Chavez would visit the school many times.

At first, Blythe public school officials warned direly that this upstart school could never match the quality of the local public school. They don't talk that way anymore; mostly what is heard now are excuses about why it is unfair to hold the local public school to the same standards as those of the ERU.

"The best thing about our school is that it's small, and it can meet the special needs of our students," Carmela said. "Nobody gets lost here. In more than twenty years, there have been only a few students we couldn't reach, even though we take kids on a first-come, first-served basis. Most of our kids go on to college, and the ones who don't go on get really good jobs and go back to serving their community. Hardly any come to us at grade level, and many come speaking only Spanish, but we get them up to grade level fast, and they all want to learn English. With everybody helping everybody else, it comes easy.

"I had one girl last year," Carmela continued, "who was eighteen, but she was only in the ninth grade. She'd always moved around with her parents,

Carmela Garnica (left), director of the Escuela de la Raza Unida in Blythe, California, with two of her students, teacher Maria Rivera (second from right), and United Farm Workers president César Chávez during one of his many visits to the school, in 1984.

between L.A., Mexico, Blythe, and Salinas. She'd gotten lost in the shuffle and was held back several times. It had really hurt her pride, and when I talked to her, I could see that she wanted more than anything else to catch up. I told her we'd give her all the special help she needed if she worked hard. She did the three years of work in one year, and she scored above average on her high school graduation exam. Now she's in college and doing well."

Sandra, a sixteen-year-old junior, came to the United States from Mexico at age seven, speaking only Spanish. Now, in perfect, unaccented English, she talks about how much the ERU has meant to her. "What's so good about the ERU is that there's always somebody to help you. It's more like a family than a school. My friends in the public schools tell me that you have to get high there or you get beat up. There's so much peer pressure to join gangs. When I graduate, I want to go to nursing school. I know I can do it, because my nephew graduated last year and he's in prelaw now, and a girlfriend of mine who graduated two years ago is doing premedical studies at UC Riverside."

The pride and joy of the ERU is Radio KERU, the student's own radio station, which is managed by teacher Maria Rivera. Maria spoke of what a motivator the station is for the kids. "KERU is the only Spanish-language station in Blythe, but after 4:00 P.M. we switch to English," she said. "The kids love being DJs, and we have a rule that they can do it only if their grades are high enough. At night, when we're broadcasting in English, we play antidrug public service announcements. Six of the adult volunteers who work with the kids on the radio are correctional officers with the two local prisons, and they're great with the kids, really letting them know what's ahead of them if they fall in with the gangs.

"During the day, when we're broadcasting in Spanish, we play singers they can identify with, like Selena. People pay to put little birthday announcements on the radio, and we make more money with the radio station than with tuition, which is only $50 a month. All the field workers in the farms along the Colorado River have their little radios strapped to their hips, and they're all listening to KERU. Much of the time, it's the parents listening to their children. They're really proud of what their kids are accomplishing, and their children's futures mean everything to them."

Radio KERU (88.5 FM), with a 250-watt transmitter, broadcasts in both English and Spanish. It is manned entirely by ERU students and community volunteers. Here, station manager Maria Rivera shares a joke with Judy Garcia, 17, a senior.

Carmela spoke of the struggle to make ends meet and keep the doors open. "I swear, by the time these kids finish high school here, we should give them diplomas in fundraising. The $50-a-month tuition we charge doesn't go very far, and we make money in all different ways: the radio station, our Ballet Folklorico, the *Tiendita* that sells snacks. We get by OK, but we need the voucher. I was on the Proposition 174 board of directors, and we still help any way we can. For example, two months ago we all went to a demonstration in Sacramento to lift the limit of 100 on the number of charter schools they allow.

"What would we do if we could get a voucher representing our fair share of the tax dollars? Man, that would be luxury to the max! We need a bigger building so we aren't limited to forty kids, and we need a real air conditioner instead of a swamp cooler so the personal computers don't break down every time it gets hot. I'd like to have a place for livestock, for 4-H projects, and I wish we had a science lab.

"People say that the voucher would mean more segregation, and I say, bull!" she continued. "The L.A. public schools are almost all minority now— how can you get any more segregated than that? People forget that farm workers' families need the voucher too. There's nothing elitist about it. We need to be united if we're ever going to get educational choice. We all have to be together. It's like the name of our school: Escuela de la Raza *Unida*. We need to really be a team, and then I know we can get educational choice in '98."

Chapter 18

A Ladder Out of Poverty: Inner-City Catholic Schools

Catholic parochial schools have long been a part of America's educational landscape, and they still enroll about half of all the private school students in our country. The United States had Catholic schools long before our first public school opened its doors, and they have educated successive waves of Irish and Italian immigrants, among many others. In the suburbs, they are still educating the sons and daughters of prosperous Catholic families, while in the inner cities, the historic Catholic commitment to educating the poor continues unabated.

The mission of these schools has often gone unnoticed by non-Catholics. In the chapter on education in Hillary Clinton's *It Takes a Village,* the First Lady offers a number of ideas on educating the poor, but says not a word about Catholic parochial schools. This is all the more curious since her husband was educated in one, an experience he has described as a key influence in his achievement of becoming a Rhodes scholar. Similarly, Jonathan Kozol, in *Savage Inequalities,* offered a searing indictment of decaying inner-city public schools but never managed a visit to one of the Catholic schools a few blocks away that are succeeding at a third of the cost.

New York City's Cardinal John O'Connor has repeatedly made the city an extraordinary offer: "Send me the lowest-performing 5 percent of your public school students, and I will educate them for $2,500 per year, less than one-third of what you are now spending. If I don't raise their test scores and lower their dropout rates, you will owe me nothing."

The public education bureaucracy's response: stony silence.

Cardinal O'Connor's challenge—which still stands—is no idle boast. In 1990 the RAND Corporation compared the performance of children from New York City's public and Catholic high schools. Only 25 percent of the public school students graduated at all, and only 16 percent took the Scholastic Aptitude Test, vs. 95 percent and 75 percent of Catholic school students, respectively. Catholic school students scored an average of 815 on the SAT. By contrast, the small "elite" of public school students who graduated and took the SAT averaged only 642 for those in neighborhood schools and 715 for those in magnet schools. And, as we have seen from James Coleman's studies (Chapter 6), these results hold up even when controlled for the families' socio-economic status.

The story, however, is much more than one of superior academic results at lower cost. The sociologist and best-selling novelist Andrew Greeley has observed in his book *Catholic High Schools and Minority Students* that, even controlling for parental background, Catholic school graduates are more likely to be racially tolerant, supportive of the equality of women, and active in their communities than their public school-educated peers. And, not surprisingly, they are happier, better-adjusted people.

The story of America's Catholic schools, inspiring though it is, has a cloud over it: their beleaguered financial circumstances. With the Church's financial resources in decline and fewer Catholics choosing to join the orders, thereby forcing the schools to rely increasingly on more highly paid lay teachers, the financial situation of many Catholic schools is precarious, especially in the inner cities.

Located in one of Oakland's more troubled neighborhoods, Saint Cyril's School on 62nd Street is a haven of safety named after the fourth-century bishop who, at least for a time, brought peace to Jerusalem. Saint Cyril's is almost entirely black, with fewer than 15 percent of its families Catholic. Most are Protestant, and a few even Muslim.

As principal Ruby Williams tours the classrooms, polite children in uniforms jump up and, in unison, sing out, "Good morning, Mrs. Williams."

Principal Ruby Williams and three of her pupils at Saint Cyril's School in Oakland, where few students are Catholic. In the background is a photo of Dr. Martin Luther King, Jr., delivering his epochal "I have a dream" speech. (Photo credit: Chantal Charbonneau)

Many rush forward to hug her. "Our kids are wonderful, aren't they!" she exclaims, holding the hands of two while another clings to her leg. "As you can see, we run a thrifty operation," she continues, gesturing at the worn carpets. "Besides myself and the teachers, the only employees are my secretary and the custodian—and he got cut back to part-time this year. I wish we had money for a computer lab or a science lab, but it just isn't there."

Mary Coons, the seventh-grade teacher, and the daughter of John and Marilyn Coons, talked about the kind of commitment needed to work at a school such as Saint Cyril's. "We don't have any support staff, so we eat lunch with the kids and watch them at recess. There's no preparation period. And, of

Students at Saint Cyril's School are able to learn in a clean, safe, healthy environment where excellence is demanded, and achieved, despite the extremely modest budget. Behind these girls is a sign listing the rewards to be had for good performance: "Verbal praise; Star after name; Free time; Note to parent; Class party."

course, we don't get paid very much. It's really rewarding, though. We start with kids with a lot of disadvantages, and they do really well. We almost always beat the state averages on examinations."

Ruby Williams described the Children's Educational Opportunity (CEO) program, sponsored mainly by Ruth Berg, wife of Everett Berg, one of the key leaders in California's Proposition 174 battle in 1993. "We started out with eight kids in the CEO private voucher program, but then Saint Benedict's closed this year and we inherited another twenty, so now we have twenty-eight. The CEO program pays $750 of the tuition for kids who otherwise wouldn't be able to enroll. Our tuition is $2,350 a year, so they have to come up with $1,600 a year themselves." The program is administered by Deborah Wright, a long-time, energetic participant in the educational choice arena and a candidate for Congress in 1994 and 1996.

Tiana Smith is a twelve-year-old seventh-grader in the CEO program who would like to be a nurse when she grows up. Her grandmother, Hazel Jones, says she couldn't be happier with Saint Cyril's. "It's a great school; the teachers have a personal relationship with the students. When my own daughter was growing up, I didn't have enough money for a school like Saint Cyril's, and we feel really blessed that the CEO program has made this possible for us. They really focus on education at Saint Cyril's. It's a year-round school with a lot of homework."

When asked whether she knew who was sponsoring the CEO scholarships, Mrs. Jones replied, "No, but I've sometimes wondered." When invited to guess, she surmised that "It must be somebody who really cares about the children."

America's Catholic parochial schools, and other schools of choice like them, are not just the best hope for inner-city children, but their *only* hope. Their time-tested approach to teaching and their compassion and concern for *every* child continue to produce miracles with astonishing regularity. Catholic schools are far from being an endangered species, but the number of students they can accommodate is declining at a slow but steady rate—at a time when the population is still growing and the need, especially in the inner cities, has never been greater.

Thanks to the willingness of the Oakland diocese to subsidize schools in which Catholics are a small minority, to the sacrifices of low-income parents who scrimp and save to pay the few hundred dollars a month toward a better future for their children, to the dedication of teachers who are willing to work for far less money than their true worth, and to the generosity of people like Ruth Berg, Saint Cyril's remains a haven in the inner city. But each fall, when the children come back to school, there are the nagging worries about whether the money will be there to bring back their part-time custodian and keep the lights turned on, or whether Saint Cyril's will go the way of Saint Benedict's and cease to exist.

What is at stake is our commitment to keeping the doors open at all of the Saint Cyril's schools of the nation, and to continue to give hope to children who otherwise would have none.

Chapter 19

La Dottoressa: Maria Montessori and Her Schools

The year was 1915, and San Francisco had invited the world to the Panama–Pacific International Exposition. Eighteen million visitors poured through the turnstiles during the nine months that the fair was open, admiring exhibits celebrating the opening of the Panama Canal, the recovery of San Francisco from the 1906 earthquake, and the newest inventions of the age. Of all the exhibits, however, a single one earned *both* of the fair's only two gold medals: the "glass house" classroom in which children were learning at their own pace, of their own free will, in a demonstration of the educational principles discovered by an Italian physician named Maria Montessori.

Who was this woman who rocketed from obscurity to achieve such stunning success as one of the greatest educators of our time?

Maria Montessori was born in a small town in eastern Italy in 1870—the same year that the duchies of Italy were united into a modern nation—of parents who had neither money nor position. Despite these humble beginnings, she possessed from an early age a deep sense of duty and purpose. At the tender age of ten, when she fell gravely ill, she told her mother, "Do not worry— I cannot die; I have too much to do."

After finishing technical school, she undertook a daring—and, for Italy, unprecedented—challenge: medical school. As the first female medical stu-

---

This chapter is adapted from an article by Alan Bonsteel in the *North American Montessori Teachers Association Journal*, August 1995.

dent ever in Italy, she was subjected to even more of the hazing and abuse that has been heaped on medical students since time immemorial. The male students would hiss and make catcalls as she passed them in the corridors, and shake her desk when she was writing. Because the medical school faculty would not let Montessori do dissections of human bodies alongside her male colleagues, she was forced to learn anatomy alone at night, among the cadavers and skeletons and human organs in jars. Sometimes in the dim light she even imagined that the cadavers were coming back to life. In the midst of her medical school trials, Montessori came to a turning point in her life that she spoke of many times in later years.

One night, alone in the dissecting room, she became overwhelmed by her "sea of troubles." In despair, she suddenly left her cadavers and resolved to seek a career less mined with difficulties. While walking home through a park, she came upon a beggar woman and her daughter of about two years of age. Although dirty and living in squalor, the child began to play with a flower, in obvious absorption with this living object of wonder. Montessori was struck by her ability to find beauty in such a simple thing while growing up in such depressing surroundings. Moved by what she had seen, and instantly realizing that the pathway to helping that child and others like her ran through the corridors and dissecting rooms of her medical school, demanding though that pathway might be, Montessori resolved that whatever it took, she would persevere and become Italy's first female physician. In that child, she had found her calling.

Soon after graduating, Montessori was made director of a school for the "hopelessly" mentally retarded. Her new charges were abandoned and forgotten young souls. They came mostly from insane asylums, where they had lived their lives in prisonlike rooms, and they were known by such degrading names as "defectives," "idiots," and "lunatics." Montessori threw herself with boundless energy into this new challenge, devoting all day to her special children and then toiling late into the night, analyzing what she had observed. She insisted on the personal dignity of even the smallest child, and she created a special environment that nurtured her children's special gifts and encouraged them to learn in the way that worked best for them: creative work with their hands and through experiential interaction. Many of Montessori's "hopeless" children learned to read and write better than "normal" children. Her miracle was hailed throughout the nation, and Italy's first female physician—by now known as *La Dottoressa*—won newfound respect.

In 1907 Montessori took her new teaching principles to "normal" children, albeit those who had grown up in extremes of poverty and neglect in a slum quarter in Rome. As she described them,

> Sixty tearful, frightened children, so shy that it was impossible to get them to speak; their faces were expressionless, with bewildered eyes as though they had never seen anything in their lives . . . poor abandoned children who had grown up in dark tumble-down cottages without anything to stimulate their minds—dejected and uncared-for.

Montessori set to work with this seemingly unpromising group, offering them an unprecedented gift: the dignity and freedom to learn at their own pace, following their own interests, in a nurturing "prepared environment." Visitors to her *Casa dei Bambini* were astounded by the obvious joy the children took in their creativity and achievement. Soon Maria Montessori was the most famous person in all of Italy, and her schools began spreading to other countries in Europe.

In 1911 the first Montessori school in America opened in Tarrytown, New York, and by 1913, the year of Montessori's first visit to the United States, there were over a hundred. An American Montessori Society was formed under the presidency of Alexander Graham Bell, with Thomas Edison and Helen Keller as founding members.

In 1915 Montessori made a second trip to the United States, where she created the glass *Casa dei Bambini* at the Pan–American Exhibition in San Francisco. Upon her arrival in the Bay Area, the *San Francisco Examiner* wrote, "Madame Montessori, while speaking in Italian, won her hearers by her charm and the warm enthusiasm with which she acknowledged California's hospitality," and declared her "the greatest figure in child education."

The day after her glass *Casa* opened on August 4, 1915 in the Palace of Education, not far from where the Palace of Fine Arts still stands, the *San*

Front-page story in the San Francisco Chronicle, *August 5, 1915, announcing the opening of what would become one of the most popular exhibits at the Panama-Pacific International Exposition.*

"The hand is the tendril of the mind," said Dr. Montessori. Here, a teacher watches her young pupil discover how to discriminate objects by size, using Montessori apparatus from the Cabinet of Geometric Shapes, Drawer of Circles.

Francisco Chronicle wrote, "The success of the Montessori theory was almost demonstrated with the initial session. The youngsters plunged into the work as though they had been coached previously. The children appeared to be oblivious to the watching crowds." The glass *Casa* was surrounded by bleachers that often overflowed with audiences so enthusiastic that the *Chronicle* likened them to "fans as warm as any home club with a winning streak ever drew inside a baseball grounds." Particularly popular was the noon lunch, prepared by the children themselves, and served with good manners and aplomb that delighted their "fans."

Along each classroom wall in the *Casa* were child-sized cupboards, each full of specially designed learning apparatus. The children were free to choose any apparatus, to work alone or with others, and to continue as long as the exercise held their attention. For example, they could play with chains of beads arranged in clusters of twos, threes, fours, and so forth. By playing with the beads, they spontaneously learned the multiplication tables. As another example, the children could play with rough-edged, tactile letters, arranging them into simple words. In time, they sometimes, in one of those magic moments of Montessori instruction, "exploded into writing," to use Montessori's term, exclaiming, "I can write! I can write! And nobody told me how!"

Maria Montessori, 1870-1952, visiting with the children at one of her schools in London in 1951. (Photo from Archive Photos/Popperfoto).

Exemplary of Montessori education in California today is the Marin Montessori School in Corte Madera.[1] Located in an enclave of educational choice near the San Francisco Bay, one can find, within a few hundred yards, the Marin Country Day School, a traditional college preparatory school; the Lycée Français bilingual immersion school; and the Allaire private school for special needs children.

Visitors to the Marin Montessori School watch in astonishment as well-behaved, courteous children work and play together intently, just as the visitors

---

[1] The board of directors of the Marin Montessori School would like it known that they do not take positions on political issues. The school's inclusion in this book indicates neither their endorsement of nor their opposition to the views expressed here.

did at Montessori's *Casa dei Bambini* in Rome in 1907 and in San Francisco in 1915. The children use traditional Montessori learning apparatus, little changed in a century, as well as more modern learning tools, such as personal computers.

The school's administrator, Jules Layman, described the special efforts the school has made to promote diversity. "Located in an affluent community as we are, we've had to work at creating a diverse student body that reflects society as a whole," she said. "We have a diversity committee of fifteen or twenty parents addressing these issues. Our tuition is higher than average for California Montessori schools, ranging from the high four thousands for the younger children to the high six thousands for our oldest kids, the sixth-graders. To help reach our goal of having a socioeconomic mix, we have a scholarship program for parents for whom the tuition would be a hardship. Last spring the diversity committee sponsored an international picnic, with the cost of admission being an ethnic dish for eight. The children begin learning Spanish with a native instructor when they are as young as four-and-a-half years old.

"Over the last five years we have seen a continuous growth in the need for before- and after-school child care," she continued, "because we're finding that in most families these days, both parents work. The facility we use for this purpose, known to the children as the clubhouse, is almost at capacity now. If this trend continues, it looks as though we may need to consider implementing an all-day Montessori program in the classrooms as one of the next steps to staying up with the times.

"We're a nonprofit organization, with governance by a ten-member board of directors, all of whom are current parents at the school," she said. "The curriculum and pedagogical decisions, however, are strictly reserved to our faculty council, with some of our teachers having been with us for fifteen to thirty years. Montessori teaching principles have served us well through the years, and that's what ultimately defines us as a school."

Montessori schools are now in operation on six continents. The contribution of the Montessori philosophy to modern childhood education was perhaps best summarized by Anna Freud, daughter of the founder of modernpsychiatry, when she wrote,

> In a *Casa dei Bambini,* for the first time the child was a master in his own house. For the first time, not the praise and disapproval of adults, but joy in the success of one's own work came into its own as a suitable impetus. Above all, not authoritarian discipline, but freedom within carefully placed limits was the principle of education.

Toward the end of Maria Montessori's life, she was showered with honors, including three nominations for the Nobel Peace Prize. At the Ninth International Montessori Congress in London in 1951, many had the premonition that they would never again see Montessori, then eighty, and some were in tears as *La Dottoressa* spoke of the bond among those who work in the service of children and of the shared journey of teachers and students.

Maria Montessori died in 1952, but she lives on through her work. Her extraordinary contributions revolutionized education, not just in Montessori schools but in many other teaching philosophies, and she transformed our vision of the child. Through her gifts to the children of this world, she is with us still, and her memory is honored by those who work for the well-being and dignity of children everywhere.

Chapter 20

Hope in the Ghetto: The Marcus Garvey School

On Slauson Avenue in South Central Los Angeles, across the street from a liquor store and a taco stand, a lime green building with red trim houses the most successful inner-city educational achievement in the United States: the Marcus Garvey School. Located in a black, working-class neighborhood, and named after the Jamaican activist who founded the Universal Negro Improvement Association, the school never turns away a student—yet its preschool-through-ninth-grade students routinely best the results of schools spending many times the $428 per month that it charges.

In Marie Stewart's preschool classroom, eager two- and three-year-olds know the bones of the body and can identify the states on a map of the United States, and four-year-olds know their ABCs in Spanish and the days of the week in Swahili. In Brenda Spencer's kindergarten class, a proud five-year-old, Khalid Bowens, reads aloud from a third-grade reader, and the other kindergartners are preparing written (cursive!) reports on a U.S. president of their choice.

Several years ago, Marcus Garvey third-graders outperformed sixth-graders from a much-vaunted Los Angeles magnet school in reading and mathematics. Results such as these are all the more startling when one considers the social and economic problems of the neighborhood. The Marcus Garvey School is just a few miles from the John Locke High School, considered by many to be the worst public school in California. Yet in stark contrast to the utter hopelessness at Locke, the Garvey school is a safe haven, where the children's humanity is affirmed and academic excellence is the norm.

Anyim Palmer, Ph.D., founder and executive director of the Marcus Garvey School in Los Angeles, which has a set a standard of excellence that few other schools anywhere can match. (Photo courtesy of the Plain Dealer Publishing Company, Cleveland.)

The school was founded in 1975 by Anyim Palmer, Ph.D., a former professor and Los Angeles public school teacher and administrator, with $20,000 from his savings. Palmer established the school after concluding that the "Board of Mis-education" had abdicated its responsibilities to inner-city children. "When I was an administrator, teachers would say, 'Why try to teach these kids? They can't learn,'" Palmer recalls. "A science teacher once told me that he was actually telling kids not to bother trying to learn. He said, 'Hey, the kids are happy. I give them all A's.' Each year the public high schools of this nation graduate thousands of black children who cannot read, write, or do simple arithmetic. As a result, they cannot seek gainful employment and are therefore driven to lives of crime. Others attempt to escape the painful reality of a miserable existence by turning to dope, and still others become the perpetual welfare recipients of this nation. Here, we don't allow them to say, 'I can't.' We get in their faces and let them know they're going to learn. We're very firm. I believe in being a strict disciplinarian."

Ten minutes later, this "strict disciplinarian" is giving a loving hug to one of his problem students who has gotten good marks in behavior all week.

The unrelenting message given to Marcus Garvey's all-black student body—hard work, ambition, and pride in their heritage—permeates the school. In the classrooms, the children study the lives of George Washington Carver and Dr. Charles Drew, the physician who perfected blood transfusions and after whom the nearby King/Drew Medical Center is named. On the walls are pictures of inspirational black leaders: Nelson Mandela being sworn in as president of South Africa; Rosa Parks, the woman who refused to move to the back of the bus; Jesse Owens winning one of his gold medals at the 1936 Olympics in Hitler's Germany; and school choice pioneer Polly Williams, who has visited the school often.

"The key to success is instilling high expectations," Palmer says, "but high expectations alone don't get the job done. If a teacher doesn't believe in a child, if he doesn't like that child, the child will fail regardless of what you tell him about the expectations. Here, our teachers don't just like our children, they *love* our children as they would their own. In twenty-one years here, I've never based my hiring of teachers on their having a teaching credential, yet there isn't a school in the nation, public or private, that can beat our results. I choose my teachers because they love the children and are dedicated to serving

A proud two-year-old preschooler at the Marcus Garvey School shows how well he has traced his letters. (Photo courtesy of the Plain Dealer Publishing Company, Cleveland.)

Fourth-grade students at the Marcus Garvey School fulfilling the dream of all parents for their children: a good, values-rich education in a safe haven, preparing them well for life as responsible, productive citizens.

the community. If Sacramento passed a law saying I had to hire only credentialed teachers, my quality would go *down,* not up, because I wouldn't be able to choose the best people any more.

"About 30 percent of the children who come here are brought by their parents because they've been labeled by public schools as having learning disabilities," Palmer continued. "The public schools get more money when they label a child as having a learning disability, and all you have to do to see that most of the children who are mislabeled with these 'disabilities' are minority children is visit a public school special education classroom. Yet we take these same students with their 'disabilities,' and they're quickly working several years ahead of grade level.

"As long as the public schools are allowed to go on the way they have been, I see no relief for our children," Palmer emphasized. "A lot of my parents are public school teachers who are reaching into their own pockets to pay our tuition. They know the public schools have a captive audience and don't have any reason to get better. They'll get better fast when our people have the voucher. We could have five schools like this in the neighborhood if we had school choice. We do what we can with our school, but not everybody can afford even our low tuition. Vouchers are the key, and we're hoping that '98 is the year."

Chapter 21

The Fighting Rabbi

It is June of 1996, and as Irene Linetskaya approaches the podium to receive her diploma from the Hebrew Academy of San Francisco, there isn't a dry eye in the house. Even the headmaster, Rabbi Pinchas Lipner, a veteran of twenty-six previous graduation ceremonies, is at times overcome by emotion. All sense that what is occurring is that rarity in our lives: a true miracle.

Irene arrived from the Soviet Union in 1991 speaking not a word of English. Both of her parents had died of cancer as a result of radiation exposure from the Chernobyl disaster, and she arrived in San Francisco with no money, living in the Mission District while going to school. Yet, despite facing every obstacle that life could throw in her path, she graduated from the Hebrew Academy as her class valedictorian, accepting her diploma in perfect, unaccented English. She went on to a full scholarship at Stanford University.

"Irene went through a lot of loss and a lot of stress, and she came here far behind academically, not even speaking English," says Rabbi Lipner. "But here, we are very close. No one gets lost here, ever. I know the students in the school, and I know most of the families. We helped Irene in every way we could, and she responded magnificently. I knew she would."

The Hebrew Academy has always gone far out of its way to help the children who most need it, but in recent years it has become famous for the large number of Jews emigrating from the former Soviet Union who come to the school in search of their heritage. They now make up 70 percent of the student body, a mission for which the school was profiled on a CNN special aired

Rabbi Pinchas Lipner, dean of the Hebrew Academy of San Francisco. A tireless advocate as well as practitioner of school choice, he is a living exemplar of its value to American society.

in November 1992. Starting with students who come to the United States from the former Soviet empire and a dozen other countries, the Hebrew Academy has established a remarkable record of sending them on to universities that read like a who's who of higher education: Harvard, Stanford, UC Berkeley, Caltech, The Sorbonne, The London School of Economics, etc.

Dima Kiper is a fourteen-year-old ninth-grader who came to the United States with his family from the town of Nizhneykamsk, near the city of Kazan in Russia, in search of opportunity in America. "At first my parents put me in a public school, but I hardly spoke any English at all, and their English as a Foreign Language program wasn't very good, so a month later my parents put me in the Hebrew Academy, which is really good at teaching English. I like it here because it's small, and I know everybody and they know me. My parents like it that they have Hebrew studies here, but the academics are more important to them, because they know I have my best chance of success here."

As Rabbi Lipner guides his visitors through the school, he stops first at a photograph of a distinguished-looking teacher surrounded by rapt students.

"Edward Teller, the physicist who developed the hydrogen bomb, taught regular monthly seminars here for ten years," Lipner says. "He doesn't have a teaching credential, so they would never let him teach in a public school. Imagine! Being a world-famous physicist who has won the Fermi Prize isn't good enough for them!" he laughs.

As he races through the school with seemingly boundless energy, the man with the fiery eyes and flowing beard known as the "Fighting Rabbi" rattles off the names of some of the Jewish leaders who have helped his school. "Yitzhak Rabin came here and spoke at a press conference on our behalf. Moshe Dayan, the hero of the 1967 war, came to a fundraiser at the Fairmont hotel to help us.

"We do everything we can to make our school open to deserving children, regardless of how much money their families have," Rabbi Lipner continues. "Twenty percent of our families are on welfare, and every student in this year's senior class, without exception, is receiving financial aid from the school. Whatever it takes, we do it. I mortgaged my own house to keep the school

Renowned theoretical physicist Edward Teller, winner of the Fermi Prize, giving a science lesson at the Hebrew Academy in 1986. He would not be allowed to teach in any public school, because he lacks a teaching credential.

going. For the last few months, we've had an ad on KCBS and KGO radio to get people to donate their used cars to the school so we can sell them as a fundraising project. Can you imagine—I've become a used car salesman. *A used car salesman!*" He laughs at this odd place to which life has taken him.

"We'd like to do even more, but it's a struggle when our families have to pay taxes for public schools that are too dangerous to use, and then pay again for tuition here. There are always deserving children whom we can't accommodate.

"I led the battle to qualify the BayCARE school choice initiative for the 1996 ballot," he continues. "We kept the issue before the voters in the press, and we filled the main hall for our rally at the Beverly Wilshire Hotel in Los Angeles. The political pressure we kept up forced Governor Wilson to propose his Opportunity Scholarships. What we've learned, though, is that we need serious money if we're going to win an election for educational choice. We need to be together, and then the checkbooks will start opening.

"This work of ours is the most important thing we could be doing with our lives," he reflected. "Our schools say a lot about what kind of society we are. And no one knows better than me the chaos in our public schools here in San Francisco and many other places. *Chaos!*" he exclaims, emphasizing his point.

"Founding the Hebrew Academy and building it to where it is today wasn't easy," he observed. "We faced a lot of opposition along the way, and many people would have been happy to see us fail. We succeeded because we had a vision. It's the same thing with educational choice—we are people with a vision. As long as we keep our thoughts on that dream, as long as it guides us, whatever others may be saying, we'll get there. We'll succeed one day because we *have* to, because we owe it to the children. And I intend to be there when that day comes."

Chapter 22

A Renaissance Man: Rudolf Steiner and the Waldorf Movement

Some say that there will never again be a Leonardo da Vinci—that the modern world is too complex for any one individual to be able to master all of the disciplines of learning. Yet, at the beginning of this century, a man named Rudolf Steiner demonstrated extraordinary mastery as a scientist, psychologist, medical healer, agronomist, architect, sculptor, painter, choreographer, author, playwright, philosopher, theologian, . . . and educator.

Despite these gifts, this giant among men never lost his humility and his common touch. At the moment that has gone down in history as the birth of the first Waldorf school, in April of 1919, Steiner had journeyed from Switzerland to address the workers at the Waldorf-Astoria factory in Stuttgart. There he found some modest financial support from the proprietor for the school he proposed to establish for their children. The workers lounged around the meeting hall in their overalls, sullen and suspicious of this do-gooder with peculiar ideas who had sat out the war in well-fed Switzerland. Between the war and the influenza epidemic of 1918, all had lost family and friends, and now they faced postwar misery and despair. Many of these workers were illiterate.

Steiner spoke simply and respectfully about the hard school of life they had endured and about their yearning for a better future for their children. He earnestly described his vision of a school that would not just teach academics, but would nurture the spirits of the children as well. He addressed their questions in the terms of the workaday world, and humbly asked for their help. Little by little, he won the hearts of his listeners. The next day, many came to

Rudolf Steiner, 1861-1925. Despite his somber demeanor in photographs, he was a kind and genial man. (Photo courtesy of Verlag am Goetheanum, Dornach, Switzerland.)

Steiner to ask whether they could enroll their children in his school, and what they could do to help. The new school had become theirs.

Rudolf Steiner, the eldest son of a railroad stationmaster, was born in 1861 on the border between Austria and Hungary in a town that is now in Croatia. Perhaps because he was at first a below-average student, he later identified deeply with children who had not yet shown their full potential.

As a young man of twenty-one, Steiner was engaged to tutor a family of four children. The youngest, a ten-year-old named Otto, was a hydrocephalic ("water on the brain") child of fragile health, and so gravely mentally retarded that he was considered uneducable. With characteristic energy, Steiner not only threw himself into the challenge of tutoring this boy, but also read all he could find about the child's medical condition—an interest that was to foreshadow his later contributions to the medical field. He succeeded so spectacularly that the boy was restored to health and ultimately went on to graduate from a university.

After receiving a degree from Vienna Technical College, one of Steiner's first jobs was to edit the scientific writings of Johann Wolfgang von Goethe, whose scientific work had been eclipsed by his literary masterpieces (but who himself regarded the former as his most significant work). Steiner enthusiastically accepted this task as a stroke of destiny. His work did much to make Goethe's scientific writings better known, and it foreshadowed his own life-long passion for the nexus between science and the humanities.

During the following years, Steiner became one of the foremost leaders in German literature, philosophy, and theology. In 1912 he founded the Anthroposophical Society—literally, "The Wisdom of Man"—and in the same year he received the gift of a building site in Dornach, Switzerland, not far from Basel, that would serve as the center for the new anthroposophical movement.

Steiner himself designed the building, which he called the *Goetheanum.* Two intersecting hemispherical domes formed the basic structure, flanked by wooden walls richly adorned with carvings. The foundation stone was laid in September 1913. Less than a year later, Europe was plunged into the "war to end all wars," but, although the workers from seventeen countries—including many that were then at war—could hear the rumbling of cannons from nearby Alsace, work never stopped on this monument to peace and learning. By the end of the war, the Goetheanum was still unfinished. Nevertheless, Steiner somehow found the time to establish the first Waldorf school in Stuttgart in 1919, inspired by these bracing lines from Goethe's *Faust:*

> *Säume nicht, dich zu erdreisten*
> *Wenn die Menge zaudern schweift;*
> *Alles kann der Edle leisten*
> *Der versteht und rasch ergreift.*

Whatever you can do, or dream you can, begin it;
Boldness has genius, power, and magic in it.

Steiner contended that the First World War had occurred as a result of faulty education, that a purely materialistic school system run by an often nationalistic state cannot teach how to resolve conflict. He envisioned that the main task of Waldorf education was to provide for human beings to attain the

Rudolf Steiner with a model of the first, ill-fated, Goetheanum in 1914. The building was destroyed by an arsonist in 1923, shortly before its completion. (Photo courtesy of Verlag am Goetheanum, Dornach, Switzerland.)

optimal degree of freedom that would enable them to fulfill themselves without interfering with the freedom of others. The Stuttgart school was thus formally known as the *Freie Waldorfschule*, with the "Free" meaning independent, particularly from authority of the state. Steiner emphasized that Waldorf schools should be run by the teachers themselves.

Progress at the first Waldorf school was initially far from smooth. Steiner would travel by train to Stuttgart almost every week to visit the fledgling school. All who knew him commented on his extraordinary ability to concentrate his attention on the person with whom he was conversing and on his uncanny insight and intuition about the thoughts and feelings of his students. He himself never seemed to appear fatigued, and he cheerfully called upon his Waldorf teachers to reserve tiredness for some other occasion! He always had a kind and encouraging word for everyone, and, although in photos he invariably had a grave countenance, he was known among his friends for his impish sense of humor. It was hard not to like him.

By 1922 the Goetheanum in Dornach was almost complete. With the building standing on a wooded hillside, the paintings on the roofs of the two cupolas and the stained-glass windows—etched and ground so as to form radiant light-pictures—gave the building an extraordinary grace and beauty.

On New Year's Eve of 1922, tragedy struck. Like all great men, Steiner had his enemies, and late that night an arsonist stole into the Goetheanum, threw kerosene on the walls, and torched the building. By the time the people of the anthroposophical community could rush to the scene, flames were shooting so high into the air that they could be glimpsed from Basel, eleven miles away. While the people gathered around the inferno, flames lit the sky and illuminated their faces. As Steiner circled the blazing building, watching his dream turned to ashes, he was heard saying to himself, *"Viele Arbeit und viele lange Jahre"*—much work and many long years.

The next morning, as Steiner addressed his distraught followers, this most determined of men refused to give the arsonist the satisfaction of having inflicted hurt. He spoke only a brief sentence about the previous night's fire, and then gave the talk he had prepared, betraying no emotion. Later that day, planning began on a new Goetheanum, this one to be built of concrete.

Today the second Goetheanum stands on the same site in Dornach as the first, so gracefully taking its place on the hilltop in the Jura Mountains that it appears ageless, as though it had always been there. The performance hall inside is home to dramas by Goethe and Shakespeare, to music by Bach and Beethoven, and to performances of the soaring, balletlike eurythmies that were choreographed by Steiner and his wife, Marie von Sivers. Dornach is now an intellectual and artistic center, but perhaps more importantly, it is the main training center for Waldorf teachers, who make the pilgrimage from all over the globe to master the educational principles developed by Steiner.

Almost unique among Waldorf-inspired schools is the Yuba River Charter School (formerly known as the Twin Ridges Alternative Charter School) in Nevada City, California. Nestled among the trees in the foothills of the Sierra Nevada, it is one of only a handful of charter schools in the entire nation based on Steiner's pedagogical principles.

Parallelogram

The area of a parallelogram is equal to the altitude (a) times the base (b).

$$A = a \cdot b \ (\text{or } A = h \cdot b.)$$

Triangle

The area of a triangle is equal to one half the altitude times the base.

$$A = \tfrac{1}{2} \, ab \ \text{or} \left(A = \tfrac{ab}{2} \right)$$

The Waldorf approach emphasizes the esthetic aspect of technical subjects. This lesson was drawn (colorfully) by a seventh-grader at the Waldorf-inspired Yuba River Charter School in Nevada City, California.

Until June of 1994, the Mariposa Waldorf School in nearby Cedar Ridge had served Nevada County, but when it faltered financially and closed, a core group of Waldorf families worked with other families in the area to take advantage of California's new charter school law and open a new school responsive to their needs. Among the founding group was teacher Carol Nimick, a former Mariposa teacher and, more recently, a teacher in the Twin Ridges school district, the sponsoring district for the Yuba River Charter School.

"Aside from the distinction of being one of the few Waldorf-inspired charter schools, the Yuba River Charter School is one of the few that is physically located outside the chartering district," she said. "We couldn't find suitable space within the geographic boundaries of our own school district, so we opened in the Nevada City school district. There's nothing in the charter school law prohibiting that; it is, at this moment, an open legal question. Many of our families came from the private Mariposa Waldorf School, but more than half came here from traditional public schools."

Almost anyone with the fortune to visit a Waldorf school is struck by the creativity of the students, and the Yuba River Charter School is no exception. The children's imaginative and expressive paintings are often striking in their precocity, and inside the classrooms, the students are absorbed in drama productions and the unique, Steiner-inspired eurythmies that he himself termed the "gymnastics of the soul." As in almost all Waldorf schools, the same teacher follows a class from the first through the eighth grade, getting to know the students with extraordinary intimacy and a lifelong bonding.

"We do call ourselves a Waldorf-*inspired* school rather than a Waldorf school," said the youthful and energetic administrator, George Hoffecker, "because we are not a member of the Association of Waldorf Schools of North America. We *have* modified certain aspects of teaching practices currently used in Waldorf schools in North America. Certain verses, songs, and festival celebrations cannot appropriately be used in a publicly funded charter school, because they might be construed to be of a religious nature.

"Everything we do here is collaborative," he continued. "There's no hierarchy. The administrator coordinates the activities of the parent council, the charter council, and the faculty council, and provides the bridge to our sponsor, the Twin Ridges school district.

"We strive to involve all our families in the life of the school," he emphasized. "At a recent all-community meeting, seventy-eight parents signed up to work on one or more of our committees. I believe it works both ways, though—when people have freely chosen a school, there is a sense of ownership that you wouldn't find otherwise." Before becoming the administrator at the Yuba River Charter School, Hoffecker taught for twelve years at the Live Oak Waldorf School in Applegate, near Auburn, and he was fortunate enough to have known the philosopher Dr. Carl Stegmann, who, as a young man of nineteen, had worked with Rudolf Steiner in Dornach.

At the time of Steiner's death in 1925, there were only a handful of Waldorf schools in existence, but the seed had taken root. Today there are over 600 Waldorf schools worldwide, and more than 100 new ones are being established every year. More than seventy-five years after the founding of the first Waldorf school, Steiner's educational philosophy has stood the test of time and is as relevant and vital today as in the beginning—a tribute to the genius and inspiration of this Renaissance man who shared our century.

Chapter 23

A School for Our Times

It's hard to know how to think about ourselves these days. On the one hand, American technology dazzles the world. Computer chips small enough to hold on a fingertip do what a mainframe did a few short years ago. Through a handset small enough to fit in a coat pocket, we can reach anyone on earth who owns a phone. Medicine is closing in on some of the most fundamental mysteries of life. Science races ahead at a dizzying pace. We are the best, we are the world's leader.

On the other hand, an appallingly high percentage of adult Americans are semiliterate or illiterate. Teenagers get pregnant, do drugs, and drop out of school at rates that would shock any other modern country. Millions of Americans are trapped in a generational cycle of poverty, and our infant mortality is a tragedy. We lock ourselves behind gated "communities," or, for the less well-to-do, we walk the streets at night in fear, careful not to stumble over the homeless. We are alienated and cynical about our most fundamental institutions. We are a third world country.

Which is the *real* America? Both.

In the Industrial Age, you walked to the factory in the community where you lived. A college education got you "ahead," but as long as you could at least read and write, you could learn a job that would usually last a lifetime.

This chapter is adapted from an editorial by Alan Bonsteel in the *San Francisco Examiner*, July 31, 1995.

The infinite richness of the world of books has opened for this little boy at the Sudbury Valley School in Framingham, Massachusetts, where children are encouraged to pursue their own interests. (Photo credit: Michael Greenberg)

A little girl at the Sudbury Valley School practices her writing. The children set their own pace, deciding what to learn and how to learn it. The results are outstanding. (Photo credit: Michael Greenberg)

In the Information Age, a home workstation is as likely as a corporate office to be a job site, and modern "road warriors" even work from their virtual offices at 30,000 feet while jetting around the globe calling on clients. Jobs undergo technological revolutions, and workers who fail to adapt are left behind—as millions are. Our communities are no longer geographic, but defined by interests and values: the Internet links us more than the town meeting. Those who can't function in this profoundly unsheltered environment can be utterly alone—as all too many are.

Although there are many factors that explain the gulf between our strengths and our weaknesses, clearly the most fundamental failure is our educational system. At a time when we need schools that can teach kids the skills that will enable them to adapt and change, our schools themselves have failed to adapt. Our science and technology are twenty-first-century, but our public schools are nineteenth-century. In most, the teacher still drones on for endless hours in front of students who are bored at best and alienated at worst.

In an era in which the average eighteen-year-old can expect to change careers at least three times before retirement, rote memory is less important than it once was; the hard disk drive can handle that better. We need people who can access information, who can think creatively, who can communicate clearly, who can work cooperatively. Beyond these skills for acquiring material success, we need people who know who they are, who have a sense of meaning and purpose in their lives, who are in touch with others, and who can build and nurture their own communities.

At the highly innovative Sudbury Valley School in Framingham, Massachusetts, there are no classes, no assignments, and no authority figures. Students are free to follow their own interests and to work cooperatively on projects with others. They are self-governing, not just in the sense of a token "student government" but in truly meaningful ways, such as making decisions about allocating the school's resources and writing the school's rules. They run the judicial process that resolves disputes and penalizes infractions.

One might think that in an atmosphere of such freedom, little real learning would take place. But in fact, kids want to make something of themselves, and, as they see the utility in what they need to know, they learn passionately and well.

The results are spectacular. A visitor to the school finds a neat and tidy campus with many students hard at play—or, if one prefers the Puritan ethic, hard at work—on computers. They enjoy being there so much that the worst punishment for a rules infraction is banishment from the school for a day. There is no alienation from their institution, because they *are* their institution. They are communicative, mature, caring, self-directed kids who know what they want. The vast majority go on to college, almost invariably to the school of their first choice. Those who don't go to college find creative, satisfying work, often running their own businesses. It is almost unheard-of for Sudbury graduates to pump gas or languish in jail. Is there a selection process that accounts for such outstanding results? Hardly; admission is first-come, first-served, and many of Sudbury's students had done poorly in stultifying public schools elsewhere.

Stuart Williams-Ley, founder of the Santa Clara Valley School in Santa Clara, California, having a discussion with fellow staffers Valerie Winterberg (left), D'Arcy Nicola (center), and a number of students. Important decisions about school affairs are reached by consensus among all concerned—children as well as adults. (Photo credit: San Jose Mercury News/Karen T. Borchers)

In many ways, the atmosphere is reminiscent of the think-tank "campuses" of Hewlett-Packard or Apple Computer. It is the wave of the future, but given Sudbury's three-decade track record, it is hardly experimental; the results are clear and repeatable. And more Sudbury-style schools have been established throughout the country, including three recently founded in California: in Sacramento, Santa Cruz, and Santa Clara.

At the Santa Clara Valley School, educational pioneer Stuart Williams-Ley, who made a stake as a Fidelity mutual fund manager and is now pursuing his dream, talked about the challenges of the first year.

"We started the year with five staff members and fifteen children, now eighteen, who represented about as diverse a group of kids as you will find anywhere. One of them, by the way, was the daughter of the noted economist and physicist Dr. David Friedman, who is himself the son of Dr. Milton

Friedman, of course one of the true giants of the educational choice movement. Many of the other children had struggled in public schools elsewhere.

"Since we're in Silicon Valley, I suppose people might think that we're in the business of training future scientists. While some of our eight-year-olds are more computer-literate than many adults, that's true of most of the Sudbury-style schools elsewhere as well. If I had to characterize the theme of the first year, it has been building our community. Communities don't just happen, and after starting with twenty people, most of whom hadn't met each other previously, we've had to work at it.

"One of the few rules established by the founders was to set up a legislative council and a judicial council to write the school rules and adjudicate disputes. In our first year, the judicial council has worked overtime, hearing as many disputes among our eighteen students as the Sudbury Valley School in Massachusetts hears in a year with ten times as many students. It has, however, been an extraordinarily important learning and community-building experience.

The youngest student at the Santa Clara Valley School concentrates on a computer, which he seems to be "conducting." The children are given ample time to try things on their own.

"We recently had a fascinating case in which a student was playing some violent video games—including one in which the victims of the violence were exclusively women—that most of the other students found objectionable," he continued. "The kids had to really wrestle with issues not just of the rights of this individual versus the rights of the community, but also of the rights of people in the larger, global community whom they, of course, had probably never met—specifically the potential victims of the violence that was encouraged by these video games.

"In the end, the students, each with the same one vote as the adults in the community, established a new school rule prohibiting acts or words denigrating or encouraging hatred toward any class of people. The debate demonstrated one of the biggest, and most subtle, advantages of our school: how students here really listen to the adults. When adults spoke, kids listened carefully, weighing the points so they could decide how to vote. This is a lot different from listening to clues about the next test. Also, having students fully involved in working out rules gives the kids a sense of ownership. Students here care about the rules, because the rules are *their* rules.

"A few days ago," Stuart continued, "I was walking down to the 7-Eleven store with one of our children, a boy who has both Tourette's syndrome, giving him a lot of tics and other involuntary mannerisms, and a fetal alcohol-like syndrome as a result of his mother's use of antiseizure medication during pregnancy. This little boy had been made a pariah in the public school he previously attended, but in our school, where everybody watches out for each other, he made friends and became part of the group. As we walked along, he said to me, 'You know, Stuart, our school is like a little town, with little businesses, and a government, and even trials. I like that.' And, after a pause, he said, 'But you know why I *really* like it here? It's because it's like I have two families, one at home and one here. I love it here.'

"As we finish our first year," Stuart added, "I think we've succeeded in establishing a community among the children here. What's happening now, though, is that the parents are being increasingly drawn into that community, with school meetings, potluck dinners, and so forth. For me, the most exciting part of my job here is that we are creating a community—a community of freedom and democracy, a place where there is dignity and respect for all."

Chapter 24

Schools of Choice as Communities

For those of us who would build a better world, the central issue is community. Is it our purpose merely to satisfy our own material needs and private gratifications, or are we all in this together, sharing the higher calling of service to a greater good? The struggle between belonging and alienation, between connectedness and drift, between meaning and emptiness, is the central drama of our lives, and a crucial factor in the success of any school.

There are certain academic skills so central to success that there is scarcely any debate over their worth: to be able to read and write our language, to master at least elementary mathematics, to know enough history to have an idea of how we got here and who we are. The evidence for the value of school choice in improving academic outcomes and imparting these skills and others is overwhelming.

For those of us who have worked for years in the field of school choice, however, and have visited as many independent schools as we have, it is clear that the fundamental character, the very essence, of schools of choice is a sense of community never found in government schools, which can compel the attendance even of the unwilling and the alienated. What we have seen, again and again, are schools of choice that are under *neighborhood* and *local* control; that are on a human scale with a human face; that take to heart E. F. Schumacher's dictum that "Small is beautiful"; and that, as Henry David Thoreau expressed it, "march to the beat of a different drummer."

This chapter is adapted from an article by Alan Bonsteel in ΣΚΟΛΕ, *the Journal of Alternative Education,* Summer 1995.

Students of different ages learn with and from each other at the Sudbury Valley School, which is the archetype of many other successful schools of choice. (Photo credit: Michael Greenberg)

As we have seen, schools of choice are about as varied as one could imagine. Some are strictly academic; others emphasize spiritual and moral instruction, and education for life. Some are uncompromisingly disciplinarian; others are as laissez faire as a school can be. Most are private schools, but, increasingly, many are public schools of choice, such as California's charter schools.

What unites this disparate group, however, is that every family attending that school is there because they have *voluntarily chosen to do so*—an absolute condition for any meaningful sense of community. In schools of choice, the students are bonded by that shared purpose, whether it be a passion for the arts, a shared heritage, or a desire for a deeper spiritual life. The families are strengthened through their involvement in the decision-making process, either through direct participation in the governance of the school or through the leverage of their right to leave if their needs and desires are not satisfied.

The teachers, for their part, enjoy greater professional satisfaction in working in a school in which the students *want* to be there and in which there is far more collegiality and far more opportunity for creativity than in government-run schools. The most important attribute of any school is the students' experience of *community*: that feeling of belonging, the camaraderie of learning, and the knowledge that not only are the teachers there for them, but their families are also involved and will be heard. It is this unique quality one finds in schools of choice that makes the battle for school choice so passionate, so much more than simply an accounting of better results at lower cost.

The evidence that school choice produces superior academic results and lower dropout rates is overwhelming, but the issue goes far beyond simply a question of quality. There is a creativity, an energy, a vitality in schools of choice. There is a commitment that comes from having freely chosen. The right to choose carries with it a dignity, a shared purpose.

Schools of choice will bring us together.

Part III

Let teachers teach,
Let children learn,
Let parents choose.

— CAMPAIGN SLOGAN OF
PROPOSITION 174

Chapter 25

The Proposition 174 Story

Alan Bonsteel

As I sat in the sound room of the Ronn Owens KGO radio talk show in San Francisco during the station break, I felt torn. On the one hand, I was handily defeating my opponent, the California Teachers Association's director of communications, Tommye Hutto, in a debate over Proposition 174, California's 1993 voucher initiative for educational choice—on Northern California's most widely broadcast radio talk show. On the other hand, I could hear on my headset the commercials being aired, and my heart sank as I realized that most of them were CTA commercials attacking Prop. 174 and repeating the same lies I had just refuted on the air. That wouldn't have been so bad if it had been only the radio debate audience they were reaching, but in the "air wars" over Prop. 174, we were being carpet-bombed by a well-financed opponent that could dominate television and radio, while we had enough money for just a few television commercials that were broadcast only in Southern California.

Despite outspending us 6-to-1, the CTA still felt it had to lie to defeat us, and Hutto was no exception to the rule. The two most flagrant lies revolved around the financing of Prop. 174, which provided that every time a student left a California public school for a private school with a $2,600 voucher, the remainder of the $5,200 annual per student spending would revert to the state treasury—from which it could, of course, be reallocated to the public schools, at the legislature's discretion. The CTA was trumpeting that the public schools would "lose" not $5,200 in funding each time a student left, but *twice* that, or $10,400, bankrupting the public school system.

The initiative also stated that current private school students would have to wait two years to be eligible for vouchers, so that the savings from public school students transferring into less expensive voucher schools would pay for the vouchers of the children who had been in private schools all along. The CTA was trumpeting that these 550,000 private school students would be *immediately* eligible for vouchers, at a cost of billions of dollars to the taxpayers—an especially absurd charge to make against an initiative that had been endorsed by every major taxpayer group in the state. The points I made on the radio were met by infuriating cackles from Hutto, but caller after caller phoned in to let her know in no uncertain terms that it was time for the CTA to start taking seriously the collapse of California's public schools.

That encounter summarized the essence of the CTA's campaign against us: raw power, money, and fraud. One would think that, with the kind of money they had with which to defeat us, they would take the high road and sell the concept of compulsory public school education on its merits. But their campaign was just one mudball after another, each charge more outrageous than the last. Unfortunately, it worked all too well.

The Prop. 174 story began with Stephen Guffanti, a San Diego-area physician who, like myself, divides his time between family practice and emergency medicine. Disturbed by the high dropout rate and the violence and drugs in our schools, he won an election in 1986 to the Vista Unified School District board—quite a feat for someone who had never previously registered to vote. Once on the school board, he was horrified by what he saw. Although he'd run for the position with the idealistic intention of improving education for the kids, he soon discovered that the Sacramento education establishment was dictating to local school districts how to run their schools, and that the school board, in fact, was almost impotent to effect any meaningful reform. The only "accountability" referred to the process of exposing the children to a curriculum, a process that required no demonstrable product.

A Vista public school teacher convinced Guffanti that a voucher system was the best solution, because it gave the economic power to the parents to choose. In August 1990, Guffanti announced to the press that he was going to place the issue on the ballot rather than seek school board reelection. The newspaper stories generated many calls from people who wanted to help, including one from Rick Arnold, a professional petition circulator now living in Carson City, Nevada, who had a personal interest in school choice. Arnold has helped to qualify voucher initiatives for the ballot in Oregon, Colorado, and Washington, and in 1988 he had attempted to qualify an educational tax credit initiative for the ballot in California. Through his organization, Californians for Quality Education, he had extensive contacts, and he introduced Guffanti to many of the key players, including John Coons and Joe Alibrandi, the warm, idealistic CEO of Whittaker Corporation in Los Angeles. Alibrandi had been a donor to our 1980–1981 effort and is a powerful public speaker for school choice, sometimes evoking moving images of the black inner-city boy from a single-parent family whom he has "adopted." And he is an accomplished writer and a natural leader. He quickly agreed that it was time to move forward on the school choice issue.

Many of the early organizing meetings were hosted by Sam Hardage of San Diego, the CEO of Hardage Suite Hotels and a former Republican candidate for governor of Kansas. He became an important financial supporter and remains one of the key movers and shakers in the educational choice movement.

Soon Mike Ford, a prominent taxpayer activist who had also worked on the 1988 effort, was brought into the rapidly expanding group. Ford was one of the cofounders of Autodesk Corporation; he is legendary as a coauthor of Prop. 140, California's term limits initiative in 1990, and for his work in many Libertarian causes. A highly intelligent individual with an easy sense of humor, he quickly saw the paramount importance of school reform.

Guffanti, Alibrandi, and Ford each made a commitment of $50,000 to get things going, and in 1991 an initiative committee was formed, with Ford as chairman, to draft a proposal for the 1992 ballot. Guffanti later closed his medical practice to devote full time to the effort—a sacrifice that was almost certainly crucial to our qualifying for the ballot. Other key people influencing the initiative draft included John Coons, Stephen Sugarman, and Milton Friedman; Manny Klausner, an attorney and long-time Libertarian leader; Michael Rothschild, head of the Bionomics Institute; David Barulich, a financial planner and policy analyst; David Harmer, an attorney and eventual author of the book *School Choice: Why*

We Need It, How We Get It[1]*;* Clint Bolick, an attorney with the Institute for Justice; and William Ball, a Pennsylvania attorney and expert on the constitutionality of school choice.

The drafting committee, unfortunately, could not reach a consensus, and Coons and Sugarman found that they were unable to support the final draft. Their objections were that (1) it allowed participating private schools to charge whatever the market would bear in extra tuition and to select the most academically promising students, thereby pitting private schools in an unequal competition with public schools, which would still be required to accept all comers without charging extra tuition, and (2) it pitted students from low-income families in an unequal competition with students from high-income families whose parents could add on thousands of dollars in extra tuition to the voucher.

Coons and Sugarman believed that a voucher of only $2,600 was large enough to pay for most existing private schools, but too small to pay for new private schools coming into existence to meet the new demand, making the voucher of little benefit to families too poor to add on extra tuition. The initiative allowed public school choice, but only with the base $2,600 voucher. Since the California Constitution prohibits public schools from charging extra tuition, Coons and Sugarman felt that this amount would have been too small to result in any new schools of choice within the public sector, again pitting the public schools against the private schools under an unequal set of rules. It did not include special education children, except to the extent that the legislature authorized them, which they considered an unlikely event, given the influence of the CTA on California politics. Coons and Sugarman detailed their reasons for nonsupport of Prop. 174 in their 1993 book, *Scholarships for Children.*[2]

At the time of this disappointing development, I was finishing my family practice residency at McGill University Medical School in Montreal, and I wouldn't meet any of the new players in the field until almost a year later, after

---

[1] David J. Harmer, *School Choice: Why We Need It, How We Get It* (Washington, DC: Cato Institute, 1994).

[2] John E. Coons and Stephen D. Sugarman, *Scholarships for Children* (Berkeley: Institute of Governmental Studies Press, University of California, 1992).

the initiative had qualified. I vividly remember, though, talking with Jack Coons on the telephone and learning how upset he was. Coons and Sugarman made it clear that they would not support this initiative; the campaign filed it with the secretary of state and continued without them. The hard-working Kevin Teasley was hired to oversee operations; he continued as the campaign director until mid-1993, when the well-known political strategist Ken Khachigian (who eventually went on to run Robert Dole's California presidential campaign) took over, and Teasley became director of fundraising.

The initiative had barely gotten off to this rocky start when it ran into a new problem, one that wasn't fully apparent at the time: election fraud. We needed to gather about one million signatures within five months to qualify for the ballot. Most of California's paid signature gatherers were organized by just two firms. One belonged to Mike Arno, whom our campaign hired. The other firm, in a move apparently unprecedented in initiative-campaign history, was hired by the CTA specifically to *disrupt* our signature-gathering effort. Arno states that he himself was offered a "retainer" of $400,000 by the public education establishment if he dropped his efforts on behalf of school reform; to his everlasting credit, he turned it down. The signature gatherers working for him were often followed by spies who alerted opponents of the initiative to their whereabouts. Squadrons of public school teachers would then come and surround the tables and harass and intimidate citizens trying to exercise their constitutional right to petition the government.[3]

To these difficulties were added the financial problems of an organization that depended entirely on the goodwill of public-spirited citizens. These problems were overcome—just in time—primarily by the arrival on the scene of business leader Everett Berg, whose major donation gave the campaign enough money to put the signature drive over the top, and by the heroic efforts of Steve Guffanti in helping to organize 220,000 volunteer signatures, without which the initiative would not have qualified.

It was only after the signatures were turned in to the secretary of state for verification, however, that the full extent of the job the public education

[3] An account of this sabotage of the electoral process was given by Charles M. Price in an article entitled "Signing for Fun and Profit: The Business of Gathering Petition Signatures," in the *California Journal*, November 1992, p. 545.

establishment had done to block parental choice came to light. It quickly became clear that, besides merely disrupting our signature gathering, someone had hired shills to sign the petitions over and over with the same phony names. San Diego County Registrar of Voters Conny McCormack commented that "We have many, many more [people] who signed seven, eight, or nine times. . . . There is clearly more fraud here than we've ever seen before." The phony names made it necessary to verify every petition name-by-name, at a cost to the California taxpayers of $600,000—more money than we had spent to collect the signatures in the first place! More importantly, it cost us two extra months, causing the campaign to miss the deadline for the 1992 election and postponing the initiative to the 1994 ballot. As it turned out, events were to move that date forward.

It was at this point, in mid-1992, that I finished my residency in Montreal and returned to California. Although Coons and Sugarman felt that they had to stay neutral, I decided that the best thing I could do for the long run was to work within the campaign, carefully keeping my reservations to myself in public forums, and arguing our case from the perspective of a coworker and colleague hoping to unite the educational choice movement for a future effort. Even though I considered this initiative to be less than ideal, I believed it would still produce an extraordinary improvement on the disaster taking place in our public schools, if it passed. Cliff Cobb, the author of *Responsive Schools, Renewed Communities,* also decided to participate to a limited extent in the campaign, with a similar strategy. I learned later that Terry Moe of the Hoover Institution, the author of *Politics, Markets, and America's Schools,* was on the phone to the major donors, telling them he could participate in a second effort only if the approach were radically altered. The above-mentioned people, along with Carlos Bonilla, eventually formed the "Sugarmoe" group of the school choice movement.

As it turned out, the problems with the drafting of the initiative cascaded into multiple problems with the political campaign. Coons, Sugarman, and I had been lobbying the Catholic bishops since the late 1970s; they were extraordinarily well-informed about the issues and have a centuries-old commitment to the education of the poor, so their decision to decline to endorse this particular initiative came as no surprise. Their neutrality on the issue put the campaign in the difficult position of trying to explain why, if this proposal was a good thing for private schools, the Catholic Church—representing about 60 percent of California's private school enrollment—was sitting on the sidelines.

The initiative put public schools, to which Americans remain deeply attached despite all their shortcomings, at enough of a disadvantage in admissions and tuition add-ons that the California Business Round Table declined to endorse it. The business community largely sat out the election, dramatically decreasing our fundraising capabilities.

Because the initiative left special education children in the public schools (barring a miracle from the legislature) and because its method of calculating per student spending potentially threatened funding for special education, the private special education schools in California, which receive public funds for about 9,000 children under the provisions of federal Public Law 94–142, did not support it.[4] They took a "neutral but concerned" stance toward the initiative through their organization, the California Association of Private Special Education Schools. And finally, the press was generally critical of the initiative draft.

I attended my first organizing meeting in Emeryville in the summer of 1992 with some misgivings. It was cochaired by Everett Berg and Mike Ford and was attended by the brilliant economist Michael Rothschild, the author of *Bionomics* and an adviser to legislators on both sides of the aisle. I quickly discovered that these were eminently likable, open-minded, public-spirited individuals with whom I would be happy to work. Unfortunately, Ford was soon to leave for Texas, for business reasons. The loss of his unparalleled experience and skill in organizing major grassroots initiative campaigns was a great blow.

With Ford's departure, "Ev" Berg became the leader of most of our Northern California efforts; I got to know him quite well and developed an enormous affection and respect for him. His business ventures encompassed, among other

---

[4] For an excellent report on this issue in California, see the article by Janet R. Beales entitled "Special Education: Expenditures and Obligations" (Los Angeles: Reason Foundation, Policy Study No. 161, July 1993).

things, a chain of retirement homes and ownership of one of the country's largest manufacturers of heating and cooling controls for buildings. I found him extraordinarily well organized and focused, but he also had an infectious sense of humor and an optimism that kept things going even in some of our darker moments. Aside from rescuing the signature drive in the nick of time, among many other contributions, it was also Berg who arranged background checks on two "witches" in Contra Costa County who claimed that they wanted to open a voucher school—and who both turned out to be former public school employees.

In the spring of 1993, Governor Pete Wilson called for a special election in November 1993 for an urgent change in tax law that needed voter approval. Under California law, all initiatives already qualified for the ballot went on that election. In fact, ours was the only one affected.

In mid-1993, some new major donors to the campaign materialized: the idealistic Howard and Roberta Ahmanson, who often spoke of their vision of a renaissance in ethics in American society and of the importance of school choice in achieving that goal, and John Walton, whose commitment to education reform has become a driving force in the school choice movement. Other important donors, too numerous to list here, came forward to help the campaign with large contributions. Ultimately, thousands of public-spirited citizens donated to this first school choice effort, and all the small contributions were equally valued and appreciated.

Our opponents, the Committee to Educate Against Vouchers, had the huge advantage of simply being able to deduct compulsory contributions from the paychecks of California's public school teachers, including many who *supported* school choice. Although many estimates of what the two sides spent have made it into print, the secretary of state's *official* campaign finance report shows the anti–Prop. 174 spending at $24.0 million, versus $3.7 million for the pro-174 side. Almost all the anti-174 spending came from compulsory payroll deductions (union dues and special assessments); if the campaign had been run on voluntary contributions, our side would have been the big spender! In fact, in October 1996, in a legal case brought by approximately 700 teachers, an arbitrator ruled that the CTA had improperly spent millions of dollars in fee money to campaign against Prop. 174 and ordered it to repay $4 million to teachers—more money than our side spent *altogether*.

The CTA also didn't hesitate to use taxpayer money to finance their campaign. Again and again, they used taxpayer-funded telephones and printing equipment to get out their message. Nor did they hesitate to use California's schoolchildren as pawns in defending the financial self-interest of the teachers and the bureaucracy: again and again, schoolchildren were forced to bring home to their parents messages opposing school choice, almost invariably printed at taxpayer expense.

One of my jobs in the campaign was to write and distribute as many editorials as possible to California newspapers—a good example of how an underfinanced campaign can compensate for lack of money. These editorials ultimately reached six million readers in the pages of some of California's largest-circulation newspapers.

To this day, I'm amazed by the weakness of the speakers put up against us by the CTA, and by what a strong effort we made, under the able direction of our speaker's bureau coordinator, nuclear physicist David Anderson. Probably our most powerful public speaker was Wilbert Smith, Ph.D., a former Pasadena school board member who, aside from his oratorical gifts, can convincingly argue the benefits of school choice to minorities, since he himself is black. By the end of the campaign, Smith's reputation was such that most CTA speakers were refusing to go up against him.

Other top speakers included the hard-hitting Joe Alibrandi himself; Laura Head, an eloquent Black Studies professor at San Francisco State University; Steve Hayward, a researcher at the Pacific Research Institute and a cutting-edge debater; Deborah Wright, who went on to run for Congress in 1994 and 1996 and who has recently founded an organization called Stop Ebonics—Educate Our Kids (SEEK); Carl Brodt, who had been an award-winning debater at the University of Santa Clara; and Steve Guffanti, the keynote speaker at both of the Northern California fundraising dinners I organized (both times earning a well-deserved standing ovation). The campaign was also honored by the public appearances on our behalf by two former U.S. secretaries of education: Lamar Alexander and William Bennett.

Especially memorable was the night that San Francisco investor Bill Oberndorf brought Polly Williams and former secretary of state George Shultz to the University Club in San Francisco to speak to a packed audience about

Williams's highly successful low-income voucher program in Milwaukee. The impact of these two speakers was enough to significantly augment the campaign's war chest.

On the speaking platform, one exchange in particular was unforgettable: the debate between Mike Arata, a key East Bay school choice leader from Danville, and Ralph Flynn, the executive director of the CTA. Held at San Francisco's Commonwealth Club, the debate was a contrast from the moment the two stepped on stage—the dynamic, energetic Arata and the tired, inarticulate Flynn. Arata had carefully prepared every word, every nuance, and utterly routed Flynn, who could only offer the vapid observation that "It has taken us a hundred years to screw up the public schools, and it will probably take us another hundred to fix them," an admission that was met with surprised laughter from the audience. Flynn left the stage ashen.

As the Spanish speakers in our group, it fell to Carlos Bonilla and me to reach the Hispanic community. After my first successful foray into this realm before 300,000 viewers on Modesto's Channel 17, I tried something that really got my adrenaline going: a Spanish-language talk show. It was the Peruvian-born Carlos de Marti's *Buenos Dias California* on *La Grande Diez-Diez* (The Big 1010), Northern California's most popular Spanish-language radio show. Since I'm often tuned to the San Francisco-based *La Grande Diez-Diez* while driving around the Bay Area, I had no trouble with de Marti's accent, but when he finally said, *"Vamos a abrir las lineas telefónicas,"* there were butterflies in my stomach. I speak Spanish all day in my emergency room, but having to field all kinds of Latin American accents over the telephone made me more than a little nervous.

I needn't have worried. Caller after caller vented their frustrations with the public school system. Some were forced into bilingual programs but wanted English-only programs for their children; others had children who had been forced into English-only programs and wanted more time for them in bilingual education. It made intuitive sense to them that *they* should be making these decisions for their children, and not the school *jefes*. All were worried about violence in California's public schools. As I left, de Marti smiled, shook my hand and said, *"Gracias, muy amable,"* and observed, "You know, I have my own four *niños* in Catholic parochial schools and it's really costing me *un montón de dinero*. I could really use those vouchers myself!"

Three months before the 1993 election, I flew to New York City for training in television speaking from Roger Ailes, the media guru who brought Ronald Reagan back from the brink of disaster after his first debate with Walter Mondale, coining the phrase, "I don't want to exploit the youth and inexperience of my opponent for political reasons." While in New York, I paid a call on Barbara Kantrowitz, *Newsweek* magazine's education editor, and persuaded her to write a story about us. She described New York City's public schools as "atrocious," and she and her husband had made great sacrifices to put their own kids in private schools. She had personally visited Holland's school choice plan, so she knew first-hand of the success of school choice programs overseas.

The story that Kantrowitz ultimately wrote, however, under the title, "Take the Money and Run," was fairly critical, characterizing Prop. 174 as callous to the disadvantaged and damaging to public schools. I felt torn that, on the one hand, I had arranged this nationwide magazine coverage, but, on the other hand, the story was generally negative. On the "third" hand, though, Kantrowitz's criticisms were some of the same ones I would have made had I been in her position, and that experience, as much as anything, convinced me that the next effort needed a much-rethought approach.

Following are what I believe to be the most important lessons we learned from this campaign and the lopsided loss that befell us.

1. A school choice initiative must aim to *improve* public schools, and must not be perceived as pitting these schools against competition they cannot survive.

Despite all the disappointments the American people have had with public schools, they are still attached to them and want to see them not just survive, but succeed. To that end, a school choice initiative must provide a level playing field between public and private schools with regard to admissions, tuition add-ons, and the accepting of special education students.

2. The voucher must be small enough not to raise taxes, but large enough to help poor people who can't add tuition to the base voucher.

In a high-spending state such as New Jersey, where public schools spend an average of over $11,000 per student per year, achieving the goal of a voucher that is large enough for the poor but small enough to avoid raising taxes could be a matter of choosing an intermediate-size voucher that meets these two conditions.

In California, however, the political calculus is more complicated. As the opposition is quick to point out, California's per student spending is below the national average. Prop. 174's $2,600 voucher was perceived by most voters as too small to pay for a private school education. But on the other hand—*if* one accepts the implausible assumptions of the state legislative analyst—it is remotely conceivable that, in the event of a much-slower-than-expected rate of transfer of students from higher-priced public schools to lower-priced private schools during the two-year phase-in period, Prop. 174 could have cost the California taxpayers a few hundred million dollars when current private school students first became eligible for vouchers. Even if this *were* true, however, it was *certainly* true that, in the long run, the initiative would have saved the taxpayers *many billions* of dollars.

The voters, and even the governor, focused on those few hundred million dollars, and Prop. 174 was criticized both coming and going, both as too small a voucher to be useful and too large a voucher to be affordable without raising taxes. As a result of this experience, one of the few uncontroversial principles in California's educational choice movement is that the next initiative will under *no* circumstances cost the voters a penny—a guarantee that will be carved in stone in the California Constitution.

In rough terms, California is now spending about $5,600 per elementary and secondary student per year, counting federal, state, county, and local contributions. Of this, about $400 is federal aid, which cannot be controlled with a state initiative—which leaves about $5,200 per student that *can* be controlled. From this $5,200 we must allocate enough to pay for vouchers for students already in private schools—about 10 percent of all students, both in California and nationwide.

So far, so good. There's a further complication, however: California's legislative analyst has pointed out that public schools must be left with enough funding to meet their bonded indebtedness *even if the number of students enrolled in public schools drops.* While everyone in the school choice movement agrees that the state must meet its obligations, all of us question why, if public schools lose students, they couldn't just rent out their empty school buildings to the new private schools coming into existence and use the income to help pay off the bonds.

The legislative analyst has also "allowed" us far less in savings from the decreased cost of new public school construction, once a voucher program is implemented, than we project. Unfortunately, our point of view has not won over the legislative analyst, whose opinions are crucial because they go into the voter's pamphlet and are quoted by the media as an unbiased and reliable analysis. In California, within the parameters the legislative analyst has allowed us, if all families received the same-size voucher, $4,000 is about the *maximum* amount that could be achieved, and then only with a phase-in period of about twenty years.

Finally, another crucial element of the calculation is that low-income students receive more state educational funding than higher-income students, because of categorical funding for such special situations as bilingual education. As of the 1994–95 school year, children in California who qualified for Aid to Families with Dependent Children received, on average, about 24 percent more state funding than children who were neither poor nor special-education. The combination of the lower percentages of low-income families already enrolling their children in private schools and the higher state funding these lower-income families receive provides a strong argument for a school choice system focused on the poor, who, after all, are the ones hurt most by the catastrophically bad schools they are forced to attend.

The calculations are complex; they depend on how many current private school students choose to participate in a voucher system and how quickly students transfer from public to private schools with vouchers. The bottom line, however, is that if we limit ourselves to the same-size voucher for all, it is difficult in California to come up with a voucher that is both large enough to help the poor and small enough not to take away per student public school funding or require new taxes. To those of us in the Sugarmoe group, a same-size-for-all voucher makes sense in California only if we scale tuition add-ons to the family's ability to pay, such that the wealthier families are generally paying more in extra tuition than poorer families. We must also bear in mind that numerous opinion polls have shown that the public believes that private school tuition is about twice its true level, a misperception the opposition can be counted on to exploit.

What *is* possible is vouchers for everybody, but larger ones for the poor; in fact, the larger vouchers for the poor are essentially "free" money because such a small percentage of the poor can now afford private schools. A low-income voucher also meets these conditions; in fact, we could probably *decrease* taxes with a low-income voucher, and we wouldn't need the long phase-in times required with a voucher plan that includes all income groups. A third possibility would be a hybrid approach in which low-income families, or those in dysfunctional public schools—who tend to be low-income—received the voucher first, followed by a slow phase-in of everyone else.

Any of these approaches could be combined with choice in the public sector. Experience has shown that very few of the children attending charter schools were lured there from existing private schools—once again easing the pain of paying for school choice for those already in the private sector. Various proposals have been floated to combine these proposals with basic reforms of public schools to make the initiative more attractive to voters, such as mandating a decrease in public school bureaucracy and putting more money into the classroom, or abolishing teacher tenure.

3. The school choice movement must be united.

As in any issue about which people feel passionately, there have been major disagreements within the school choice movement about the ideal approach to a voucher initiative. This is hardly surprising, considering the complexities of the issue. Yet even if we're united, we'll always go into battle outnumbered and outgunned. We can't afford to be fighting among ourselves.

The last-minute opinion polls in the Prop. 174 campaign showed us losing, but the final tally in November 1993 was even worse than the polls had indicated: our side lost by more than a 2-to-1 margin. There were many long faces at campaign headquarters the next morning. In retrospect, though, it's clear that Prop. 174 advanced the cause of school choice enormously, both in California and nationwide. Aside from the publicity already mentioned, we received extensive national coverage in the *Wall Street Journal;* one of my own articles was published in the *National Review;* and we even received some international publicity in the form of an article in Britain's *Economist.* Although it was a great disappointment that the popular vote was not more encouraging, the campaign did familiarize the voters with the issue of school choice, and it organized school choice advocates.

Perhaps more importantly, though, Prop. 174's qualification for the ballot posed a threat that forced the public school establishment to acquiesce to the experiment of allowing 100 charter schools in California. This allowed the establishment—hypocritically—to claim that they, too, were in favor of educational choice. Charter schools are far from perfect: there are too few of them, even now enrolling fewer than $1/2$ percent of California's public school students; they are too bureaucratically controlled; and they offer choice only within the public school sector, so innovation is limited, and schools offering spiritually based instruction are not permitted. But there is enough of an element of school choice in them that, even with far less funding than traditional public schools, they are already starting to pull away from the pack.

I am moved when I visit these charter schools. For years, those of us who were in the school choice movement from the beginning had to content ourselves with incremental changes in public opinion. Now we have real schools of choice for kids who otherwise would have been left out. We have real school buildings in which real students are learning—kids you can talk to, kids whose lives have taken a turn for the better because of the devotion of a handful of determined school choice activists. The results are there for all to see. With far less money, the charter schools are, beyond question, producing better results than traditional public schools.

Those of us in the educational choice movement put our blood, sweat, and tears into making those 100 charter schools a reality, and, if we have to, we'll go to the barricades to defend them. These schools are the ram's horn of Joshua that will one day bring the walls of Jericho tumbling down.

Chapter 26

Free Market, Fair Market

John E. Coons

The exchange of viewpoints in this chapter and the next, by two individuals widely acknowledged as preeminent in the field of educational choice in the United States, continues a debate that began more than thirty years ago, when John Coons was a professor of law at Northwestern University and Milton Friedman was a professor of economics at the University of Chicago.

The California Family Choice Initiative was conceived in the summer of 1978, then developed in collaboration with the U.S. Representative who had volunteered to be its official sponsor and fundraiser. That November, Leo Ryan was to die tragically in Guyana. The signature drive fell short, leaving untested the political prospects for any scheme of school choice that is focused upon ordinary and low-income families. During the 1980s, the content of voucher initiatives around the country became more strongly influenced by Libertarian thinking. Several of that design were to be crushed at the polls successively in Michigan, the District of Columbia, Oregon, Colorado—and finally, in 1993—California, with Proposition 174.

Reflecting upon this accumulating and uniform experience, most supporters of choice have turned to legislation conceived in the spirit of 1978. The Wisconsin story is the most familiar; there Democratic legislators and a Republican governor jointly produced for Milwaukee a highly popular program of scholarships for low-income children. Even unfriendly critics concede the experiment to be a success. Similar programs were adopted in Puerto Rico and Cleveland, Ohio. And in many states, children "at risk" are now subsidized to attend private schools just at they were before federal subsidies transmogrified the many forms of special education. Finally, a renaissance may be dawning in California itself. In 1996 Governor Wilson narrowly missed legislative enactment of his program of choice for educationally disadvantaged children, but his plan received praise from formerly hostile media, and, indeed, no serious criticism has appeared from any responsible source.

The "private voucher" has also made its appearance with a focus upon the poor. In January 1990, the California Institute for Educational Choice was formed to encourage philanthropists in large cities to underwrite scholarships expendable in inner-city private schools. Responsive programs sprang up in twenty-eight major cities, all confining their charity to low-income families. These private initiatives have been welcomed by every part of the political spectrum.

In designing systems of choice, what is clear as never before is that no more than 30 percent of the electorate favors a general system of unregulated uniform vouchers that are available to children of all income classes. If a critical mass of Democratic and centrist Republican voters is to be recruited for school choice in California, the emphasis upon the poor must first be restored. Unfortunately, while the continuing cadre of activists who favor that emphasis is large enough to frustrate pure Libertarian proposals, it is insufficient to proceed to the ballot on its own. Indeed, the general population and the press seem unaware that the distinctive aim of this established group of reformers is to favor disadvantaged children. Before *any* version of choice can receive a fair hearing after Prop. 174, the uncommitted core of California voters will somehow need to learn that—properly designed—choice can represent both the common good and a special opportunity for poor families. And those pure market enthusiasts who have worked so nobly for choice will either make it a common cause or leave the concept a parlor game for economists.

In search of unity, the ever expanding 1978 group has responded to Libertarian and conservative colleagues over the years with a variety of accommodations. Admission of applicants by lottery was abandoned; tuition add-ons were embraced; separate information vouchers were scrapped; due process rights of students were converted to contract; the private schools' right to enforce church attendance was affirmed; and so forth. Sometimes—as on the question of testing—the centrists have been persuaded first to favor, then to reject, specific positions; they remain content to switch wherever it is plausible that fairness and efficiency may lie on either side. Finally, they have on occasion simply changed their own minds; Libertarian and conservative friends have taught them a thing or two, and, no doubt, will teach them more. Nonetheless, when the chips have been down, those in the center have been excluded from the critical moments of the drafting process, and the emerging proposals have been wholly unacceptable to the ordinary voter, the poor, the media—indeed, anyone not committed to the *Market über Alles.*

At its polar right, the school choice movement consists of intelligent, good-hearted people. On other political issues, many of these dedicated reformers have shown a practical turn; none deliberately wastes his or her time and treasure on political nonsense. Few betray a subconscious need to play the lemming. Thus, regarding vouchers, one would expect them to seek allies—if not the 1978 crew, at least other, more amiable, representatives of the center. They might well discover an occasional Democrat who actually cares for ordinary people and the poor. In any case, their hope for a pure laissez faire treatment of the children of the poor has been rejected by both the voters and every mainline institution, including such important players as the Catholic church and the California Business Round Table; it may be time to revisit the issue of strategy.

These political errors, if such they be, are neither surprising nor discrediting. As an esthetic and powerful ideology, the market can come to seem an end in itself—even *the* end, defining the content of the good. Such false transcendence, however, is potentially tragic. For all its captivating qualities (I agree it is beautiful), the market is but a tool whose worth is to be judged by its capacity to serve specific ends. The list of benign human purposes that it advances can seem endless; nonetheless, the market remains an instrument and never a proper object of worship. In economics, as elsewhere, idolatry is risky: the idols are fickle.

Sometimes they curse us by obscuring the obvious. Although the market has won popular assent as the primary regulator, there remains the clear exception of education. Here the issue of consumer choice continues to be unsettled. A public that has been receptive to competition and deregulation in air commerce and telecommunications is, on this one question of the schools, deeply skeptical. Even discounting the baneful effects of union deceit (and presidential hypocrisy), vouchers remain a hard sell to the very voters who have embraced all other market reforms. Has idolatry blinded the enthusiast to problems that bother the amateur?

In these few pages my answer must be simple, hence wrong in detail. Happily, my distinguished mentor and friend, Milton Friedman, will be around to correct me, as will his and my common opponents: the operators of the educartel. My opinions, which appear to be shared by the skittish core of the American electorate, will thus receive healthy criticism from opposite ideological poles. It is this set of specific popular beliefs that has kept the ordinary citizen in a state of prudent suspension; he is perplexed as he watches both the monopolists and the pure marketeers avoid the center, leaving the mass of us in an intellectual no-man's-land.

Here is the heart of the public's wisdom on the question of schools: The chief objectives of any benign educational policy are moral and social; the market may be their efficient vehicle, but never an end in itself. Any proposed reform will be judged in part by its apparent capacity to deliver higher test scores, but even more by its promise (1) to lodge responsibility in poor and ordinary families, and (2) to engender trust among diverse social groups. Further, given 150 years of the familiar monopoly, choice bears the burden of showing that it will better serve these two broad social goals.

These popular concerns imply a number of technical criteria. The most salient are seven. *First,* public schools must not be disfavored; they must be given the degree of freedom that is to be recognized for private schools. Though Libertarians might prefer to end government schools altogether, voters reject this notion out of hand. Paradoxically, they do so for a sound economic reason: so long as there are consumers who prefer them, market theory itself *requires* these schools. Further, government providers are easily accommodated within a market structure; Stephen Sugarman and I have specified several different legal arrangements that would allow their instant formation in deregulated form by the local school boards, cities, universities, teachers, and parents. I do not refer here to "charter" schools of the bureaucratic and minimalistic sort presently allowed in California. Only a *voucher* system operating on the same rules in *both* sectors can provide the flexibility necessary to effective participation by public schools.

Second, the private school must be protected from regulation of every activity that is important to its identity. Of course, it must teach the "basics" that are now required of private schools (English, math, history, etc.). Beyond this—apart from a proscription of criminality and group hatred—the school should be free to teach what it pleases and to hire the teachers it wants, on terms fixed freely by contract. Relations between the school and the family should be conceived in similar terms. So long as parents are forewarned, the school should be free to set its own standards of discipline and academic advancement. There may be other aspects of "identity" that deserve protection; on this all of us are open to argument. Here, again, I see no irreconcilable conflict.

By the way, in a market composed of public and private schools—all in competition with one another—unions would at last function in the economy of schools as they do in the private sector generally. The crucial change for the teachers unions would be that the nonrich customers of the employer (the school) would no longer be conscripted and forced to accept whatever the school dished out. The freedom of families to transfer—and thus to endanger the school (and the jobs)—would at last provide the unions an incentive to be prudent and restrained. School choice is pro-union in the best sense that it aims to normalize the balance of power among customers, providers, teachers, and unions. We should all be quick to say so.

Third, the new system must ensure that private providers who accept tax money from parents share the primary purpose of the new system, namely, authentic autonomy and responsibility for those families who presently lack choice. The achievement of this public good may require a participating private school to enroll, as a small proportion of the student body, children whom it might prefer to exclude on financial or academic grounds. These children would be identified by their eligibility for federal programs. The lowest proportion of such pupils that has been suggested is 15 percent, the highest, 25 percent. The rule would apply only to new students, and only to the extent that the school received applications from eligible children.

No proposal has been more popular in the opinion surveys, and none less popular with market purists. In 1991 and again in 1994, pollsters engaged by the latter carefully mangled and manipulated the questions put to their respondents in an effort to produce an overall hostile response to any preference for the poor. For example, in the fall of 1994 the crucial survey of 2,000 respondents included a question about whether the new law should include a certain provision respecting admissions and add-on tuition. The provision was stated in the following form, eliciting the responses indicated:

50a. A participating school would be required to set aside 15 percent of its new spaces every year for qualified students from lower-income families, and to accept the state *scholarship* as full payment for their tuition.

63.0%	1	*Should* be required
25.4%	2	Should *not* be required
7.4%	3	Doesn't matter/I'm opposed anyway [do not read]
4.2%	99	Unsure/dk [do not read]

As these results began to accumulate, the pollsters (whether at their own instigation I cannot say) decided to complicate the question. The last third of the 2,000 respondents (a total of 677) were given an admissions/add-on question in the following new form, with the results indicated:

67a. A participating school would have the right to dismiss students who fail to live up to its standards. Suppose each participating school would be required to *set aside,* or *reserve,* 15 percent of its new spaces every year for qualified students from *lower-income* families, accepting the state *scholarship* or *grant* as *payment in full* from lower-income families, regardless of the school's tuition amount. Other families, *not* lower-income, would have to pay the tuition amount above the state *scholarship* or *grant.* On that 1-to-6 scale we've been using, how would you rate this idea, with *one* meaning *you don't like it at all,* and *six* meaning *you like it a lot?*

19.5%	1	One/don't like it at all
12.0%	2	Two
16.0%	3	Three
21.4%	4	Four
13.6%	5	Five
12.2%	6	Six/like a lot
5.4%	99	Unsure/dk [do not read]

Consider, first, the beginning sentence that was added to Question 67a. What would be its effect upon persons who had responded positively to 50a? Such respondents might well switch to the negative on 67a—not because they opposed the admission rule, but because they opposed the broadly stated right of the school to dismiss. They could want *more,* not less, protection for the child. Thus, their negative response to 67a would in no way reduce, but only underscore, their support for the provision described in 50a.

In truth, of course, we can never know. The *primary* effect of Question 67a was to produce an uninterpretable response. Every pollster knows that, the greater the complexity, the more cautious the answers. Indeed, it is surprising that, in spite of this blatant thumb on the scale, fewer than half of the 677 surveyed responded in categories 1, 2, or 3. In any case, the one really important (and discrediting) revelation from 67a is not the respondents' ambiguous answers, but the pollsters' anxiety to conceal the existence of the consensus that had been exposed by the original question. Whatever the question reveals about voters, it speaks volumes about pollsters.

Polls aside, consider the practical question at stake here. Would it threaten a school's identity if 15 percent of each year's *new* admissions were to come from disadvantaged families? We should be clear that, under this hypothetical rule, the school could (1) recruit a pool of low-income applicants and admit those whom it preferred; (2) impose its full curriculum on all students;

(3) counsel parents against enrolling the child; (4) deny any applicant who had a bad behavioral record or a need for special education that the school could not serve; and (5) dismiss the enrolled pupil who was unruly or an academic failure. What it could *not* do is refuse a chance to that normal child of the poor whose chosen school in a given year received fewer than 15 percent of its new applications from low-income families. Would this constitute an identity crisis for the school? It has not been so for the majority of existing private schools, which, as an act of social responsibility, have already informally attempted what is contemplated by this rule—and with meager financial resources.

To be sure, the ordinary citizen also thinks that private schools that accept public vouchers ought not to price the family out. Admission would be meaningless to the ordinary family if it had to pay an extra $5,000 per child. Of course, we might make vouchers for the poor larger; even at 80 percent of public school expenditure, this would be costless, for roughly 90 percent of the poor are now in public schools. Nevertheless, this will not help if the school charges the poor family a substantial tuition in addition to the voucher. The technical solutions to this problem range from flat prohibitions of add-on tuition (too rigid for me) to a general norm that tuition must be scaled according to family means (as is now the practice in many private schools). Such price discrimination is ideologically troubling to some Libertarians; the public and the media, however, see it differently, and so must we if there is to be any serious reform. By the way, the *Los Angeles Times* has made it clear that these protections for the poor are a precondition to its editorial approval; we could, I suppose, remain above such considerations—above and alone.

I have heard the response that schools in the inner cities will not, in fact, charge their students extra, so everything will be OK. Accepting the factual premise, what would the California public think of a system of choice in which the schools in the inner cities (serving pupils of the greatest need) spent only the amount of the voucher, while those in the suburbs spent the voucher *plus* another $3,000 to $5,000 in tuition? I think I know. (Even our state supreme court might find that one interesting.) If any doubt remains of the public's view, it should be ascertained by a survey conducted with professional candor.

Fourth, the voucher must be large enough to ensure capital investment by those providers who would locate in areas where most of their probable customers could not add substantially to the voucher. A number of states have considered proposals for potential subsidies in amounts less than $3,000. These would help to fill empty spaces in existing inner-city religious schools, but they will not build many new ones. This was a specific defect of Proposition 174. To be sure, in any scheme that would provide subsidies across the board to *all* families, regardless of their wealth, a delicate judgment must be made about the size of the voucher. The amount must be small enough that the state saves money with each transfer from the traditional public school, and these savings must be large enough to provide vouchers for those who are *now* enrolled in private school—all this without materially adding to the total public cost of education. If the voucher (at least for ordinary and low-income families) must at the same time be large enough to stimulate investment in new schools, this requires a nice balancing act. Twenty-five years of confronting this problem convinces me that an appropriate technical solution can be agreed upon by supporters of choice. This problem is, of course, avoided altogether by those proposals in which the voucher is limited to the poor, for most such families are now enrolled in the public sector, where expenditure per pupil is much higher than the average private tuition.

Fifth, the public would prefer to focus the subsidy where choice is most needed. For example, a state grant that is restricted to the poorest families has already proved popular in various states. And there has been no critical reaction by the California public to Governor Wilson's proposal to subsidize choice for children now enrolled in the worst public schools. The formerly hostile *San Francisco Chronicle* and *San Francisco Examiner* even praised the idea. Such limited, and largely unregulated, proposals could finesse the internecine conflicts of choice supporters. In *Free to Choose,* Friedman himself recognized the governing principle:

> One advantage of a voucher plan is that it would encourage a gradual move toward greater direct parental financing. . . . public financing of hardship cases might remain, but that is a far different matter than having the government finance a school system for 90 percent of the children. . . .

I agree. The "hardship cases"—those families who cannot afford to pay the full cost of private school tuition—are the appropriate beneficiaries. Friedman has reconfirmed this view by his recent approval of the focused voucher used in the Milwaukee experiment. By the way, the Milwaukee system also includes a lottery for admissions and a total prohibition of tuition add-ons. With Friedman, we in the political middle endorse that program. Let me once again emphasize, however, that the regulation of admissions and add-on tuition diminishes in importance where the state subsidy is confined to poor families, for such programs can only diminish the relative educational disadvantage of these children. More and more, I am convinced that the diverse partisans of choice will most easily find common ground in such a focused— and costless—proposal.

Surprisingly, the more Libertarian supporters of choice have historically tended to disfavor any subsidy that is confined to the families who need it most, preferring a uniform voucher for all. It might be useful, therefore, to touch briefly upon the moral and social imperatives that, for the ordinary citizen, require this distinction between rich and poor. With few exceptions, children of school age have no personal wealth: all are technically poor. Their opportunity, if any, for formal schooling consists in a subsidy from either family or government. Given the natural affection of parents and their superior judgment of the child's needs, the education of children could well be left to the family wherever the family can afford it. There is no compelling moral or social argument requiring the state's provision of free education to the rich. It is only the child of the ordinary and, especially, the poor family who requires state subsidy. And that requirement is proportional to the family's need. A thoroughly rational system of choice would thus provide aid according to the family's per child wealth, and only to those families who need it. I would add the obvious point that the common objections to redistribution do not apply to children at all, for they are incapable of autonomy and are in no way responsible for having been born into poverty.

I have nonetheless heard Libertarian friends label vouchers for the poor as just another "entitlement." In light of their readiness to entitle *all* children to the same school subsidy, regardless of family wealth, I find this objection puzzling. Indeed, my perplexity is compounded when I consider that a progressive voucher could materially *reduce the universal dollar entitlement* now represented in the state education budget. I must be missing something. Could our historic disagreements on this issue be mere misunderstandings that we can at last set aside as we prepare to wrestle with the real problems?

Sixth, a neglected question that vexes the ordinary voter is what happens to special education students under a voucher system. Granting that a large number of children are so classified merely to attract state and federal money, the truly disabled child generally needs more. Happily, the solution is utterly simple and costless. Federal law guarantees the child an appropriate "Individual Educational Plan." In a state voucher system, the parents would have the new opportunity to take 80 percent of the cost of the IEP and find a private placement that is for them preferable to that offered by the government schools. Reformers might still divide over the definition of the pool of those qualified for special education, but disagreements on that question are quite independent of one's view of choice.

Seventh, the ordinary citizen is as sensitive as any free market economist to the claims of human liberty. The citizen, however, supposes that some social restraints upon the human will—and even some benefits to certain classes (such as children)—can represent an overall net gain in personal liberty. He will, therefore, give a fair hearing to the kind of legal controls upon market behavior that claim their justification in liberty itself. The man in the street exercises no irrebuttable presumption that every law is poisonous to autonomy and personal responsibility. His skepticism on this point leaves him puzzled by the kind of arguments that rely on market orthodoxy; such abstract claims are to him merely plausible and anything but self-evident. He hungers for details of the practical effects upon ordinary people of specific proposals for choice.

Surveying the rest of the planet, our typical citizen observes that those societies that have actually instituted parental choice have, without exception, rejected anything resembling a pure market model. The Dutch, Danes, British, Japanese, Russians, Swedes—you name it—all have created systems that respect and subsidize parental preference. None is a pristine market model; all focus on protection of the child as constituting a higher social priority than the achievement of frictionless competition. In my judgment, the level of regulation in these systems tends to be excessive—in some cases grossly so—and even self-defeating. Californians are a different lot and will insist upon a nearer approximation to the pure market; after all, in 1993 30 percent of them voted for virtually unregulated choice. The "yes" votes of the other necessary 21 percent, however, will depend upon the specific features that I have already described.

In these final pages, I will be a bit more specific about the *moral* and *social* changes that the public will want to hear about as the plausible outcomes of any serious school reform. In the coming national debate, reformers should stress these outcomes as the specific fruits of choice. Standing distinct from legitimate expectations of increased economic efficiency, these more humanistic consequences are of two sorts. One is the restoration of parental responsibility, with all that this entails for the family; the other is the harmonization of disparate cultural and religious groups. Choice builds family responsibility, and it nourishes the social cohesion that is so badly damaged by the present system.

First, then, consider the effect of choice upon the family itself. Given a society like our own, the imposition of a state school monopoly is a primary source of pathology for the ordinary family. The parent of average means observes that the rich are able to function *qua* family with ample authority to choose the form and content of schooling; the rest have no such authority. Their children are conscripted for state schools by strangers, regardless of parental preference. The effect of this subordination of the family upon the mind of the child is catastrophic. The adult who for five years has been champion, hero, guide, and advocate stands helpless to guarantee the child's needs. The child loses confidence in father and mother, who in turn lose confidence in themselves. Left impotent by the state, the family ceases to regard itself as the locus of authority. The parents are morally diminished in their own perception—and in that of the child.

The specific therapy for this injury to the family is society's clear confirmation of the parental prerogative. School choice reverses the course of this moral disorder, replacing insult with respect and restoring the capacity of the ordinary family to undertake for its own children what the state has hitherto confined to the rich. No more is wealth alone to be respected while poverty is drafted to serve the goals fixed by bureaucracy.

It is no secret that trust begets self-confidence, competence, and responsibility. If society wishes to recruit the ordinary family to play its part in forging a more civil community, it must begin by expressing, not contempt for, but confidence in, the family's judgment regarding its own children. Family choice is an invitation to the disaffected to connect once again to every aspect of responsible citizenship. All supporters of choice ought to be able to agree on this, but such talk of family rejuvenation has in fact come hard to marketeers. Perhaps a fascination with economic theory has obscured the benign social implications of their own cherished individualism.

Nor have the purists among them even begun to emphasize the healing potential of choice for the discord of jarring groups—racial, ethnic, cultural, and religious. The present regime of schools has ensured nothing but mutual mistrust. The educational melting pot might have been sane policy in a century when America had a common moral culture; in our present state of pluralism, it is sheer nonsense. Any common curriculum, by definition, is impossible. Any canon of studies imposed by government will be either (1) some *private* model of the good life—one designed by the bureaucrat who happens to be in charge—or (2) the wholly vacuous "vanilla" curriculum that emerges from the political lobbying process. It will not be the curriculum of the "people," for the people are in agreement on only two things: parental responsibility and the dignity of the family. In America, there is no social definition of the content of the good life.

In such a society, the imposition of school assignments and compulsory curricula upon ordinary families is an act of hubris. It is small wonder that racial, cultural, and ideological identities get bruised and insulted. Differences— including race—that, in a community formed by choice can be interesting and synergistic, are rendered threatening by government force. Choice is the specific instrument of intergroup harmony. It is precisely as the individual becomes empowered to continue or discontinue a particular relation that he becomes free to experiment. So it is that private, low-budget schools serving ordinary families produce stable interracial communities. Because no one *has* to be there, everyone is content to be there. If there is a hope for racial and cultural integration, surely it lies in the liberation of those families who will act freely as social pioneers, demonstrating that the waters are safe.

No free market economist denies these psychological and social propositions, but virtually none so far has deployed them in political argument. There are professional explanations for this neglect, but, if the marketeers wish to persuade the bulk of American voters that choice is a good thing, they may need to embrace and express this broader view of the issue. Political hope lies in a coalition of family-oriented Democrats and free-market Republicans— and vice versa—united in support of a mechanism that directs help where help is needed. For my part, I would commit to any of the following devices (always assuming that the details of drafting do not betray its central purpose):

1. An unregulated voucher exclusively for lower-income families, expendable in both public and private schools (including religious schools).

2. The #1 model coupled with an empowerment of the legislature to extend the voucher to *all* families on terms that protect the ordinary family from government-initiated wealth discrimination.

3. The #1 model but with the class of beneficiaries defined as some specific subpopulation of children who are educationally disadvantaged (by some condition other than, or in addition to, family poverty).

4. A general system of vouchers for all children, but with appropriate protections against government-initiated disadvantage by relative family poverty. There has been some talk of employing a lottery among a school's applicants to fill half its places. This could be a plausible compromise.

These, of course, are merely examples. I would emphasize that any system, to be acceptable, must ensure that neither private nor public schools are excluded or disadvantaged. Competition must be fair among all providers.

The established players in this very serious game of school reform bear an awesome responsibility to the children and families of California. Considerable statesmanship will be necessary to conceive, bear, and deliver an initiative for choice that is acceptable to the voter in the middle. Nevertheless, we must try once again. I hope that collaboration is possible. I am certain only that it is necessary.

Chapter 27

Programs for the Poor Are Poor Programs

Milton Friedman

I agree with almost everything that Jack Coons says in the preceding chapter. We have the same objectives. Where we disagree is on the best way to attain those objectives: whether by a system that contains special provisions tailored specifically for children from low-income families or by one that treats all children alike.

Jack stresses the political appeal of special provisions for children from low-income families. I do not disagree with him. Low-income vouchers are politically popular, and for a good reason. As Rose and I wrote in 1980, "The residents of the inner cities are probably more disadvantaged in respect of the level of schooling they can get for their children than in any other area of life, with the possible exception of crime protection—another 'service' that is provided by government."[1]

Yet I am persuaded that a direct attack on the problems of children of low-income families will serve them less well than an indirect attack. That conclusion derives from a lesson that I learned more than a quarter of a century ago in the course of a debate on Social Security with Wilbur Cohen, one of its fathers and a former Secretary of what was then the Department of Health, Education, and Welfare (HEW).

---

[1] Milton Friedman and Rose D. Friedman, *Free to Choose* (New York: Harcourt Brace Jovanovich, 1980), 158.

I criticized our Social Security system for transferring income from low-income to middle- and upper-income groups. Cohen replied, "I think he is probably right about that. But that is part of the system's political sagacity. . . . I am convinced that, in the United States, a program that deals only with the poor will end up being a poor program. There is every evidence that this is true. Ever since the Elizabethan Poor Law of 1601, programs only for the poor have been lousy, no good, *poor* programs. And a program that is only for the poor—one that has nothing in it for the middle income and the upper income—is, in the long run, a program the American public won't support. This is why I think one must try to find a way to link the interests of all classes in these programs."[2] A truly profound observation. I have yet to find an exception to his adage that "A program for the poor will be a poor program."

It is tempting to suppose that low-income vouchers could be the entering wedge to a general voucher program. But apply Wilbur Cohen's insight. Suppose a low-income voucher program were adopted, as it has been in Milwaukee and Cleveland. The unions have not taken that lying down. They have been fighting both in the courts. But suppose they lose, those programs go into effect, and are expanded from their present limited scope to include *all* low-income families. The well-meaning advocates who supported the programs out of concern for the poor would believe that their purpose had been accomplished and move on to other things. But the unions would not go away, and they would move to control the voucher-accepting private schools, or at least to reduce the effectiveness of their competition. The obvious route is through seemingly innocent regulations constraining the freedom of private schools to hire, to teach, and to conduct their business in other ways. The unions are past masters at the exertion of this kind of legislative intervention. And who would oppose them? The politically weak lower-income families? The voucher-accepting schools? They might succeed, but Wilbur Cohen's insight suggests that they would not.

Contrast this situation with a voucher that treats all families alike. It will, in Wilbur Cohen's words, appeal to "the middle-income and the upper-income" families. Equally important, such an unrestricted voucher would generate

---

[2] Wilbur J. Cohen and Milton Friedman, *Social Security: Universal or Selective?* (Washington, DC: American Enterprise Institute for Public Policy Research, 1972), 54–55.

a broad, heterogeneous market for education that would attract new schools of all kinds: religious, nonprofit secular, private for profit. A new, innovative, major industry would arise that would compete effectively with the public schools, force them to improve, and offer a real counterweight to the unions.

Let me make a more general point. Throughout history, innovations and improvements that have started out benefiting the wealthy have ended up with the poor as the major beneficiaries. Consider a few examples from modern times. The automobile began as a very expensive luxury; so did television. Had it not been for the well-to-do who could afford such luxuries, neither industry would ever have gotten the initial customers they needed to survive. Yet both products became "necessities" that benefit almost all members of society. The same is true of the telephone, radio, air travel, microwave oven— you name it. In education, too, the poor will benefit most from arrangements that give the greatest scope to innovation and experimentation, which is what a large, competitive, private educational market will provide.

But, Jack may say, you are being utopian. Low-income vouchers may be politically feasible; universal vouchers are not. Perhaps so, but this is, at the least, unproved. I thoroughly disagree with his contention that a low-income voucher would have fared better in California in 1993 than Proposition 174 did. Polls showed majority support for 174 until the unions launched a concentrated barrage of falsehoods and misstatements backed by a treasure chest some six times what the proponents could muster. Under the circumstances, I thought it was remarkable that we got the support of as many as 30 percent of the voters. A Coons-type voucher might have produced a different set of falsehoods and misstatements by the unions, but it would not have reduced their opposition or the treasure they could muster. The end result would have been the same.

As Gilbert & Sullivan put it: *Faint heart never won fair lady!/ Nothing venture, nothing win/ . . . In for a penny, in for a pound.*

Chapter 28

Public Schools: Make Them Private

Milton Friedman

The following essay was first published as a guest editorial in *The Washington Post* on February 19, 1995. The final sentence refers to the BayCARE voucher initiative of 1995–1996, which fell short of the signatures needed to qualify for the California ballot. Copyright © *The Washington Post.*

Our elementary and secondary educational system needs to be radically reconstructed. That need arises in the first instance from the defects of our current system. But it has been greatly reinforced by some of the consequences of the technological and political revolutions of the past few decades. Those revolutions promise a major increase in world output, but they also threaten advanced countries with serious social conflict arising from a widening gap between the incomes of the highly skilled (cognitive elite) and the unskilled.

A radical reconstruction of the educational system has the potential of staving off social conflict while at the same time strengthening the growth in living standards made possible by the new technology and the increasingly global market. In my view, such a radical reconstruction can be achieved only by privatizing a major segment of the educational system—i.e., by enabling a private, for-profit industry to develop that will provide a wide variety of learning opportunities and offer effective competition to public schools. Such a reconstruction cannot come about overnight. It inevitably must be gradual.

The most feasible way to bring about a gradual yet substantial transfer from government to private enterprise is to enact in each state a voucher system that enables parents to choose freely the schools their children attend. I first proposed such a voucher system 40 years ago.

Many attempts have been made in the years since to adopt educational vouchers. With minor exceptions, no one has succeeded in getting a voucher system adopted, thanks primarily to the political power of the school establishment, more recently reinforced by the National Education Association and the American Federation of Teachers, together the strongest political lobbying body in the United States.

(1) The Deterioration of Schooling

The quality of schooling is far worse today than it was in 1955. There is no respect in which inhabitants of a low-income neighborhood are so disadvantaged as in the kind of schooling they can get for their children. The reason is partly the deterioration of our central cities, partly the increased centralization of public schools, as evidenced by the decline in the number of school districts from 55,000 in 1955 to 15,000 in 1992. Along with centralization has come—as both cause and effect—the growing strength of teach-

creasing violence, lower performance, and demoralized students and teachers.

These changes in our educational system have clearly strengthened the need for basic reform. But they have also strengthened the obstacles to the kind of sweeping reform that could be produced by an effective voucher system. The teachers unions are bitterly opposed to any reform that lessens their own power, and they have acquired enormous political and financial strength that they are prepared to devote to defeating any attempt to adopt a voucher system. The latest example is the defeat of Proposition 174 in California in 1993.

(2) The New Industrial Revolution

A radical reconstruction of our educational system has been made more urgent by the twin revolutions that have occurred within the past few decades: a

---

About 90 percent of our kids now go to so-called public schools, which are really not public at all but simply private fiefs primarily of the administrators and the union officials.

---

ers unions. Whatever the reason, the fact of deterioration of elementary and secondary schools is not disputable.

The system over time has become more defective as it has become more centralized. Power has moved from the local community to the school district to the state, and to the federal government. About 90 percent of our kids now go to so-called public schools, which are really not public at all but simply private fiefs primarily of the administrators and the union officials.

We all know the dismal results: some relatively good government schools in high-income suburbs and communities; very poor government schools in our inner cities, with high dropout rates, in-

technological revolution—the development, in particular, of more effective and efficient methods of communication, transportation, and transmission of data—and a political revolution that has widened the influence of the technological revolution.

The fall of the Berlin Wall was the most dramatic event of the political revolution. But it was not necessarily the most important event. For example, communism is not dead in China and has not collapsed. And yet beginning in 1976, premier Deng initiated a revolution within China that led to its being opened up to the rest of the world. Similarly, a political revolution took place in Latin America that, over the course of the past several decades, has led to a major increase in the fraction of people there who live in countries that can properly be described as democracies rather than military dictatorships and that are striving to enter open world markets.

The technological revolution has made it possible for a company located anywhere in the world to use resources located anywhere in the world, to produce a product anywhere in the world, to be sold anywhere in the world. It's impossible to say, "This is an American car" or "This is a Japanese car," and the same goes for many other products.

The possibility for labor and capital anywhere to cooperate with labor and capital anywhere else had dramatic effects even before the political revolution took over. It meant that there was a large supply of relatively low-wage labor to cooperate with capital from the advanced countries, capital in the form of physical capital, but perhaps even more important, capital in the form of human capital—of skills, of knowledge, of techniques, of training.

Before the political revolution came along, this international linkage of labor, capital, and know-how had already led to a rapid expansion in world trade, to the growth of multinational companies, and to a hitherto unimaginable degree of prosperity in such formerly underdeveloped countries in East Asia as the "Four Tigers." Chile was the first to benefit from these developments in Latin America, but its example soon spread to Mexico, Argentina, and other countries in the region. In Asia, the latest to embark on a program of market reform is India.

The political revolution greatly reinforced the technological revolution in two different ways. First, it added greatly to the pool of low-wage, yet not necessarily unskilled, labor that could be tapped for cooperation with labor and capital from the advanced countries. The fall of the Iron Curtain added perhaps a half-billion people, and China close to a billion, freed at least partly to engage in capitalist acts with people elsewhere.

Second, the political revolution discredited the idea of central planning. It led everywhere to greater confidence in market mechanisms as opposed to central control by government. And that in turn fostered international trade and international cooperation.

These two revolutions offer the opportunity for a major industrial revolution comparable to that which occurred 200 years ago—also spread by technological developments and freedom to trade. In those 200 years, world output grew more than in the preceding 2,000. That record could be exceeded in the next two centuries if the peoples of the world take full advantage of their new opportunities.

(3) Wage Differentials

The twin revolutions have produced higher wages and incomes for almost all classes in the underdeveloped countries. The effect has been somewhat different in the advanced countries. The greatly increased ratio of low-cost labor to capital has raised the wages of highly skilled labor and the return on physical capital but has put downward pressure on the wages of low-skilled labor. The result has been a sharp widening in the differential between the wages of highly skilled and low-skilled labor in the United States and other advanced countries.

If the widening of the wage differential is allowed to proceed unchecked, it threatens to create within our own country a social problem of major proportions. We shall not be willing to see a group of our population move into third world conditions at the same time that another group of our population becomes increasingly well off. Such stratification is a recipe for social disaster. The pressure to avoid it by protectionist and other similar measures will be irresistible.

(4) Education

So far, our educational system has been adding to the tendency to stratification. Yet it is the only major force in sight capable of offsetting that tendency. Innate intelligence undoubtedly plays a teach children in the same way that we did 200 years ago: one teacher in front of a bunch of kids in a closed room. The availability of computers has changed the situation, but not fundamentally. Computers are being added to public schools, but they are typically not being used in an imaginative and innovative way.

I believe that the only way to make a major improvement in our educational system is through privatization to the point at which a substantial fraction of all educational services are rendered to individuals by private enterprises. Nothing else will destroy or even greatly weaken the power of the current educational establishment—a necessary precondition for radical improvement in our educational system. And nothing

> There is enormous room for improvement in our educational system.... We essentially teach children in the same way that we did 200 years ago: one teacher in front of a bunch of kids in a closed room.

major role in determining the opportunities open to individuals. Yet it is by no means the only human quality that is important, as numerous examples demonstrate. Unfortunately, our current educational system does little to enable either low-IQ or high-IQ individuals to make the most of other qualities. Yet that is the way to offset the tendencies to stratification. A greatly improved educational system can do more than anything else to limit the harm to our social stability from a permanent and large underclass.

There is enormous room for improvement in our educational system. Hardly any activity in the United States is technically more backward. We essentially else will provide the public schools with the competition that will force them to improve in order to hold their clientele.

No one can predict in advance the direction that a truly free-market educational system would take. We know from the experience of every other industry how imaginative competitive free enterprise can be, what new products and services can be introduced, how driven it is to satisfy the customers— that is what we need in education. We know how the telephone industry has been revolutionized by opening it to competition; how fax has begun to undermine the postal monopoly in first-class mail; how UPS, Federal Express, and many other private enterprises have transformed package and message delivery and, on the strictly private level, how competition from Japan has transformed the domestic automobile industry.

The private schools that 10 percent of children now attend consist of a few elite schools serving at high cost a tiny fraction of the population, and many mostly parochial nonprofit schools able to compete with government schools by charging low fees made possible by the dedicated services of many of the teachers and subsidies from the sponsoring institutions. These private schools do provide a superior education for a small fraction of the children, but they are not in a position to make innovative changes. For

who are now entitled to send their children to government schools, and second that the voucher, though less than the government now spends per pupil on education, be large enough to cover the costs of a private profit-making school offering a high-quality education. If that is achieved, there will in addition be a substantial number of families that will be willing and able to supplement the voucher in order to get an even higher quality of education. As in all cases, the innovations in the "luxury" product will soon spread to the basic product.

For this image to be realized, it is essential that no conditions be attached to the acceptance of vouchers that interfere with the freedom of private enterprisers to experiment, to explore, and

> Everybody, except a small group of vested interests, will win: parents, students, dedicated teachers, taxpayers— for whom the cost of the educational system will decline—and especially the residents of central cities.

that, we need a much larger and more vigorous private enterprise system.

The problem is how to get from here to there. Vouchers are not an end in themselves; they are a means to make a transition from a government to a market system. The deterioration of our school system and the stratification arising out of the new industrial revolution have made privatization of education far more urgent and important than it was 40 years ago.

Vouchers can promote rapid privatization only if they create a large demand for private schools to constitute a real incentive for entrepreneurs to enter the industry. That requires first that the voucher be universal, available to all

to innovate. If this image is realized, everybody, except a small group of vested interests, will win: parents, students, dedicated teachers, taxpayers—for whom the cost of the educational system will decline—and especially the residents of central cities, who will have a real alternative to the wretched schools so many of their children are now forced to attend.

The business community has a major interest in expanding the pool of well-schooled potential employees and in maintaining a free society with open trade and expanding markets around the world. Both objectives would be promoted by the right kind of voucher system.

Finally, as in every other area in which there has been extensive privatization, the privatization of schooling would produce a new, highly active and profitable private industry that would provide a real opportunity for many talented people who are currently deterred from entering the teaching profession by the dreadful state of so many of our schools.

This is not a federal issue. Schooling is and should remain primarily a local responsibility. Support for free choice of schools has been growing rapidly and cannot be held back indefinitely by the vested interests of the unions and educational bureaucracy. I sense that we are on the verge of a breakthrough in one state or another, which will then sweep like a wildfire through the rest of the country as it demonstrates its effectiveness.

To get a majority of the public to support a general and substantial voucher, we must structure the proposal so that (1) it is simple and straightforward so as to be comprehensible to the voter, and (2) guarantees that the proposal will not add to the tax burden in any way but will rather reduce net government spending on education. A group of us in California has produced a tentative proposition that meets these conditions. The prospects for getting sufficient backing to have a real chance of passing such a proposition in 1996 are bright.

Chapter 29

Safe Sex, Safe Religion

John E. Coons

Doctors Bonsteel and Bonilla want this book (inevitably, the "BonBon book") to contain a brief comment on the significance of including (or excluding) religious education as one of the goods purchasable by parents under a system of subsidized choice. There appear to be three questions: (1) Is the inclusion of religious choice politically feasible? (2) Does any constitution require or forbid it? (3) Is it a good idea? The first two questions call for broad judgments about probability, allowing me to be brief. And once we have answered them, the third virtually answers itself. For, once we are past the technical legal issue, religion is an idea to be treated like any other. To exclude it would be a simple absurdity.

The *political wisdom* of including religious choice could well vary from state to state. Concentrations of Catholics and of particular forms of Protestant and Jewish belief will naturally affect voting patterns—in both directions. Of course, quite apart from diverse confessional attitudes, religious choice faces a dead-weight political negative in the modern forms of bias against religion itself: the sub-acid condescension of the media and the candid contempt of the academy have become personified in that paradox of the Enlightenment, the intellectual know-nothing. Few within these theophobic fraternities are likely to celebrate any increase in the ordinary family's access to religious ideas.

On the other hand, today we witness for the first time Christian churches of the most contrary theologies making common political cause. As they begin to grasp that confessional competitors are the least of their enemies, some even seem to be enjoying the experience. The pace of this shift in attitude is remarkable. Six years ago, Wisconsin legislators assured me privately that their Protestant constituents would bury them if they supported the inclusion of religious schools (mostly Catholic) in the pending Milwaukee experiment. Today, but for vexatious litigation by the teachers union, those schools would— by popular demand—be part of the legislated package.

In California (and nationally) the more professionally conducted polls have supported the religious option, at least where the particular proposals under scrutiny have appeared to deal fairly with the public schools. Indeed, many of the respondents seem prepared to *oppose* choice itself if religion were *excluded.* They could have reason to do so: an exclusively secular charter school movement could be the *coup de grâce* to formal religious education for most families. I would be interested to learn how religious school users in the state of Washington voted on the November 1996 proposal for secular charters.

In any case, the prudent reformer will think twice before flouting the values of those families who now use—and those who *would* use—religious schools. First of all, it would be fatuous to assume that the scant 10 percent now choosing those schools represent only that same small proportion of school parents who would show up to vote. Given their average economic status and their rate of civic participation, private school parents could well constitute a significant share of the ballots cast. Moreover, those presently using public schools, but seeking the same opportunity, could be even more numerous. Together these two groups of parents may constitute enough of the voting public to hold a veto over any plan that would exclude religion.

This crucial aggregation will be augmented by many nonparents, as the public generally becomes familiar with the literature that, for the first time, is systematically reporting the social effects of religious schools. A primary barrier to choice has been the sheer ignorance—hence honest reservations—of the public (and media) about what religious schools actually do. This innocence has been carefully nourished by teacher union canards ranging from segregation academies to schools run by witches and Nazis. Few citizens have the foggiest idea of the social roles played by the church schools in the inner city; how could they possibly appreciate the number of disadvantaged children whose Baptist beliefs have been carefully protected in urban Catholic schools by the generosity of suburban Catholics? And why should they not imagine—as they have been told—that religious schools have more money to spend than public schools? Such mythologies can be laid to rest, and that process has now begun. The intellectual ammunition is now available for an unrelenting campaign to inform the disinformed, thereby making religious schools an even stronger positive factor in the political calculus of choice.

Notice that I was able to say all this without once falling back on the foundational economic reality that these religious schools—Lutheran, Episcopal, Catholic, Hasidic, and others—are already in place; they represent available places in numbers sufficient to assure the market a measure of dynamism from the very start.

Now let me give the *legal question* its brief airing. This is not a technical book, and little need be said about the doctrinal apparatus that governs the church-state issue. In any case, the rules have long been both incoherent and in a state of flux. For the time being, sadly, predictions of outcomes in individual cases will necessarily depend more upon who sits on which court than upon the intellectual forms in which opinions are cast. At the level of the United States Supreme Court, the reelection of President Clinton could well shift the balance against inclusion of religious schools; whether this occurs in fact will turn upon imponderables such as the continued health and energy of certain justices now sitting. If the case were there today—and if the law under scrutiny were well drafted and fair—religious choice would prevail. But the case is not there today.

At the level of the state supreme courts, our question would require fifty different predictions, few of which I would be competent to make. First, however, let us be clear about the relation of state to federal law on our question. Under the present interpretations of the *federal* constitution, the states are probably free to forgo what the federal law would allow in respect of subsidizing religious choice. If so, there are likely to be barriers to choice in the laws of various states; paradoxically, some of these impediments will exist despite the enthusiasm of a majority of voters in a given state for inclusion of the religious option. For these are state constitutional barriers, the amendment of which, in some states, will require great political patience and the assembling of supermajorities of voters. Most state constitutions contain a religion clause fabricated amidst the nineteenth-century alarums against "Rum, Romanism, and Rebellion." These provisions were drafted with the specific intent to disadvantage the religions of the barbarian immigrants from the European continent while simultaneously maintaining mainline Protestantism as the culture of the public schools. The words of these xenophobic devices have been interpreted in widely varying ways; in California the supreme court in the 1980s disallowed the lending of fourteen dollars' worth of purely secular books to any child enrolled in a religious school. The Wisconsin and Ohio courts, now pondering the scope of their own constitutions, may well reach very different conclusions.

However the fifty state constitutions may be interpreted, about half of them can be amended by popular initiative. We in California intend to use that process to finesse the legal issue about allowing the choice of religious schools. That is, any initiative will be drafted as a state constitutional amendment to eliminate all barriers of this sort other than those imposed by the United States Supreme Court under the federal constitution. It is fair to conclude that, with a little luck, constitutional hurdles to subsidized choice of religious education will be rare among the states and wholly absent at the federal level.

There is even the ultimate possibility of a national right that religion *not* be deliberately excluded from any system of subsidized choice. Assume that the federal court *permits* the states to finance parental choice of religious schools. Assume, further, that the New Jersey Legislature then adopts a system of school vouchers that explicitly *excludes* choice of religious schools. It will be arguable that the federal constitution forbids this exclusion. For the state to distinguish in this manner between sacred and secular could either constitute a fatal discrimination against religion or a forbidden act of ideological censorship under the speech clause of the First Amendment. This is by no means a self-evident outcome, and, again, more depends on judicial politics than on logic. But such a right against religious discrimination within a system of choice represents a worthy aspiration for lawyers of the next millennium.

Finally, we come to the *question of substance:* Would subsidized choice of religious schools serve justice and the common good? Perhaps to the readers' surprise, I will offer no account of the educational and social benefits that many suppose are produced by the study of theology, the practice of prayer, and the emphasis upon responsibility to a higher purpose. Nor will I report any of the multiplying findings of sociology, all converging to the conclusion that low-budget religious schools are graduating smart, loyal, and tolerant citizens, even—or especially—when their students come from the most disadvantaged backgrounds.

I have chosen to ignore every specification of the social superiority of religious schools for this good reason: *Once it is decided that its inclusion is constitutional, there is simply no justification to exclude the religious choice as such.* To give it a disfavored status, its opponents must first demonstrate some substantial civic danger from its inclusion. A very strong burden of proof would rest upon any state that offered parents choice among every idea except belief in God. Religion does not have to prove its civic worthiness to any secular watchdog in order to join phonics, self-esteem, cubism, safe sex, unionism, capitalism, evolution, new math, Shakespeare, and Maya Angelou as things worthy to be taught. If there is some case to be made that religion is a social menace, by all means—as with any other idea—let that case be made. If not, let its opponents teach their ideas to their own children and accord me the same courtesy.

Let me put this another way. Apart from hurdles that might—or might not—be imagined by judges to constitute part of our organic law, in the USA there can be no *Index of Notions Disfavored by Superior Minds.* We are a pluralistic people with many ideas of the good life and the truth that underlies it. Some are religious ideas, some not. Some, I firmly believe, are much better than others, in the quaint and reactionary sense that they more closely approximate what in fact is the truth. But their ultimate harmony with reality is in any case not an insight that is available to either the state or any caste of secular pundits. At the extreme, of course, the state can make exceptions. It could refuse its financial support to the choice of any schools (including religious schools) that teach flat-Earth geography, group hatred, or terrorist techniques. But if it would exclude the choice of religion *qua religion,* it will need (at the very least) a justifying consensus; and, of course, none exists.

For my part, giving the child a glimpse of an authority beyond the naked human will is precisely what invites him freely to choose (or reject) responsibility to an authentic order of the good. This invitation is the well-spring of civic duty and specific therapy for the pathetic encouragement from educators to do it "my way." Nevertheless, even if I considered the civic contributions of religious teaching to be as dubious as those of "values clarification," the point would hold. Spare us the condescending concession that teaching love of neighbor is as benign as the teaching of safe sex. Religion deserves neither special benefit nor burdens. It deserves an even break.

Chapter 30

Freedom of Schooling as a Human Right

The strongest argument for giving the government a monopoly on public education—in fact, the *only* argument that makes any sense—is the notion of Horace Mann that it is the government's proper role to impose on its citizens a set of common values that would allow them to live together in a democracy. In this view, it is a nation's right to shape the attitudes of children through a common government school in order that the state might establish a stable social order and preserve its culture and its democratic institutions.

The problem, of course, is *whose* values are to be taught and *whose* culture is to be preserved. Over a century ago, the philosopher John Stuart Mill, writing in *On Liberty,* warned of the dangers of giving government a monopoly on education. Totalitarian governments, in particular, have never tolerated independent schools for long, because they are havens of free expression in societies that try to control and repress open discourse.

In a free society such as the United States, public schools are in an almost unique position, along with the armed forces and a mere handful of other institutions, in having the authority to coerce beliefs. Day after day, for thirteen long years, they may repeat a particular viewpoint and even compel students to produce the "correct" answers on examination papers. It is therefore of more than academic interest how our society chooses the values that will be taught. In the end, public schools must either opt for the tyranny of the majority, in which the many impose their values on the few, or hope to offend no one by sticking to the trite and the superficial.

In a controversial subject such as sex education, for example, public schools cannot offer explicit instruction, for fear of offending some citizens, nor may they cross the line of church/state separation and advocate a religiously based moral imperative for abstinence. The result is kids growing up with neither knowledge nor values; we see the toll every day in teenage pregnancies and sexually transmitted diseases.

For our ethnic minorities, freedom in schooling means the right to keep alive their culture, their language, and sometimes even their very identity. Certainly one of the greatest tragedies visited upon the United States by public schools has been the repression of Native American culture and language. For many years, the Bureau of Indian Affairs forced Native Americans into public schools in which their languages were prohibited and their culture denigrated in a misguided attempt to "Americanize" them. The result is that much of Native American culture has been lost forever, and many Native American languages are dying, spoken mostly by the older generation and soon to be heard only on tape recordings kept in museums. While the error of this policy has since been realized and partly reversed, the damage to pride, heritage, and even identity has been done—damage that would never have occurred had Native Americans been free to choose their destiny in community-run schools appropriate to their needs and desires.

If the government does indeed have a right to impose its values on its citizens, why not take this philosophy to its logical conclusion? Why not abolish the system of educational choice we now enjoy at the higher education level and replace it with a system of compulsory government-run universities? Why not establish government-run newspapers and radio and television stations to give us the information we "need" to coexist in a democracy? Why not a government-run church, so that we might all have common ethical values and beliefs?

In fact, freedom of choice in education is so widely recognized as a fundamental human right that in many countries it is codified into law. At least four nations—Holland, Germany, Spain, and Ireland—have enshrined in their constitutions freedom of choice in education as a fundamental human right. The 1947 United Nations Declaration of Universal Human Rights establishes the right of the family to direct the education of its children as an *inalienable right,* as does the 1984 charter of the European Community.

Nothing can be more precious than children. They embody our hopes, our dreams, our aspirations. The argument for the freedom of the family to safeguard and protect the best interest of the child is therefore stronger than in almost any other domain of the law.

Our effort is a fight on behalf of all the square pegs that society tries to force into round holes. It is a battle for freedom of expression and a renaissance in ethical values. It is a war for fundamental human rights and for dignity and freedom of choice for all.

Chapter 31

School Choice Throughout the Nation

Carlos A. Bonilla

Never doubt that a small group of thoughtful, committed people can change the world; indeed, it is the only thing that ever has.

— Margaret Mead

Our book may focus on California, but the momentum toward school choice is sweeping the nation, and at last count there were organized citizens' movements for school choice in more than thirty states. In this chapter we will mention six of the more prominent efforts—not including the Polly Williams voucher program in Milwaukee, which is the subject of Chapter 2. Two of these efforts have resulted in at least limited school choice programs at the elementary and secondary levels, and several appear to be on the verge of establishing universal statewide choice systems. While the six we profile here are among the best known, it is possible that a statewide movement not mentioned here will pull off a surprise performance and be the first to achieve what we have all been working for these many years: a statewide system of school choice that will serve as a model for the rest of the nation.

The oldest school choice program by far in the United States is the little-known Vermont program, in existence since 1869. Although the Vermont Department of Education claims not to know how many students are participating in the program, it encompasses at least several thousand students in a state with a population of over half a million. The program is perhaps best described in Cliff Cobb's *Responsive Schools, Renewed Communities:*

> With the approval of the local school board, parents may elect to send their children to a government school in another district or an independent school, in or out of state. The school board then contributes a sum equal at least to the average cost of tuition at a Vermont unified high school, while parents assume all extra costs. The governing boards of 95 out of 246 towns follow this procedure instead of building their own high schools or joining a unified high school district.
>
> The policy is not a true voucher system because it restricts choices to schools approved by the local school board, and the board has the right to reject a parent's request to send a child to an alternative school. In some cases, a town requires all of the students in its jurisdiction to attend a nearby nongovernment school. In other cases, the town allows parents to choose. About one-fourth of the ninety-five towns have vouchers that apply to elementary school as well as high school. . . .
>
> The Vermont program has worked well for over a hundred years without controversy or any of the catastrophic consequences predicted by opponents of public funds for private schools in other states. In fact, some families moving into the state have deliberately located in townships that have a voucher system.

The nation's newest school choice program to include private schools is in Cleveland, where the doors were opened in the fall of 1996 to 1,855 low-income children at the kindergarten to third-grade level. Their parents may use the voucher at any school of their choice, including religious schools. The long, hard effort to gain this toehold on educational freedom was led by long-time Cleveland City Councilwoman Fannie M. Lewis, with the assistance of school board member Genevieve Mitchell and other prominent members of Cleveland's black community.

Not surprisingly, the National Education Association had sued to try to nip this program in the bud. In July 1996, however, Franklin County Common Pleas Judge Lisa Sadler ruled against local NEA affiliates and allowed the program to begin, finding that it does not violate the Ohio or federal constitutions. Immediately following Judge Sadler's ruling, opponents sought an emergency injunction in the Ohio Court of Appeals, but in August the three-judge panel delivered a unanimous decision rejecting the injunction. The Cleveland school choice program has already been so successful that, in his State of the State address on January 14, 1997, Ohio Governor George Voinovich announced that he would lead efforts to expand it.

In September 1993, the Commonwealth of Puerto Rico established a low-income school choice program encompassing both public and private schools—the third in the nation to do so, after the Vermont and Milwaukee programs. All families with incomes below $18,000 were eligible for a voucher worth $1,500 per year. In the first year, 1,800 students used the vouchers to transfer to a school of their choice. In the second year, participation in the highly popular program rocketed to 17,000, and the public school teachers unions acted quickly to put an end to these new options for students who had previously been trapped in substandard schools. In November 1994, the Puerto Rico Supreme Court struck down the program because of an apparent conflict with Puerto Rico's constitution. Because the decision was based on the narrow grounds of a clause in that constitution, it does not affect the legality of other school choice programs under the United States Constitution.

In the District of Columbia in January 1996, the United States House of Representatives passed a limited voucher program that would have been worth $3,000 for students below the poverty level and $1,500 for students up to 80 percent above the poverty level—in a school system that spent an average of $8,100 per student in the school year 1991–92, well above the national average of $6,984. Although proponents were able to muster fifty-four votes in the Senate, a solid majority, the measure was killed by a threatened filibuster led by Senator Ted Kennedy, who had sent *all* of his children to private schools. Overriding the filibuster would have taken sixty votes, which were not forthcoming. Our nation's capitol continues to have among the worst schools in the country, with a dropout rate greater than 40 percent and school violence so pervasive that hardly any senators or representatives dare to enroll their own children in the District's public schools.

New Jersey has been a hotbed of educational choice activity, in part because it has among the nation's worst public schools, despite spending more than any other state: over $11,000 per student per year. Mayor Bret Schundler of Jersey City was elected to office in 1992 on a pro-school-choice platform, even though he is a white Republican in a city that is overwhelmingly black and Democratic. Thus far, the local NEA affiliate has succeeded in thwarting his efforts, even though *50 percent* of their own members who live in Jersey City send their children to private schools (compared with 34 percent for the general public in that city and 10 percent for the nation as a whole). At the state level, Governor Christine Todd Whitman has supported a bill for a pilot school choice program that was introduced in October 1996 in the New Jersey Assembly.

Finally, the most recent statewide initiative effort was in Washington on the November 1996 ballot, for which *two* school choice measures had qualified: one a charter school proposal and the other a voucher initiative for private schools. These two efforts were opposed, in a 2-to-1 spending blitz, by the local NEA affiliate, the Washington Education Association (WEA). According to stories in the *Seattle Post–Intelligencer* of November 16, 1996, and the *Seattle Times* of November 20, 1996, the WEA illegally concealed more than $330,000 in contributions to the anti-school-choice campaign. Both newspapers reported that most of this money had been raised by mandatory paycheck deductions from teachers.

These forced "contributions" to political campaigns that many of the teachers oppose are illegal in Washington under Initiative 134, passed by the voters in 1992. It is a much-needed law that has not yet been passed in California. Don Brazier, the chairman of Washington's Public Disclosure Commission—the state's equivalent of California's Fair Political Practices Commission—described the violations as "an absolute travesty," and the commission referred the matter to the state attorney general, Christine Gregoire, for prosecution. With characteristic foresight, the many-tentacled WEA had contributed $1,100 to Gregoire's campaign in June of 1996. To her credit, however, she returned the money in October, when she learned of the massive campaign-law violations. On February 12, 1997, Attorney General Gregoire filed a lawsuit charging that the WEA failed to correctly report hundreds of thousands of dollars in contributions for political activities, and that it improperly collected and spent union dues to finance political purposes. The WEA also organized public school teachers to coerce children to carry home illegal "Vote No" letters to their parents on the day before the election.

Both school choice measures lost by a 64–36 margin. Postelection polling, however, showed that 45 percent of the voters had voted "yes" for one *or* the other measure. Thus, had the two school choice groups been able to unite their efforts before qualifying for the ballot, they might have lost the election by only about 55–45 in their first time on the ballot in Washington—or they might have won.

The school choice movement is one of the most diverse in the United States today. It crosses party lines of Democrats, Republicans, Libertarians, Reforms, and others; it represents every ethnic group in the nation; it includes both secular humanists and the deeply religious; and its supporters range from wealthy entrepreneurs to destitute inner-city dwellers robbed of their future by dysfunctional government schools. For some, the issue is one of improved quality through open competition; for others, it is a battle for the fundamental human right to choose the schools for one's children; still others have a vision of school choice as the opportunity for our nation to experience a renaissance in ideals through schools of choice that can once again teach enduring ethical and spiritual values.

Given this diversity, it is not surprising that the school choice movement has often been contentious, and at times marred by infighting that has handed victory to our opponents on a silver platter. It is instructive to remember that, midway through the Philadelphia Constitutional Convention of 1787, the delegates were not just deadlocked, but at each others' throats. Yet they somehow rose to the occasion and recognized that the future of the nation was more important than any one individual. They persevered to create a document that is widely recognized as one of the greatest achievements of human intellectual history—a constitution that serves as a model for the world and that has served us well in both war and peace.

We now stand on the verge of a statewide school choice victory that will be a breakthrough for the nation. Which state's effort will earn the honor of being the first remains to be seen, but what *is* certain is that, when we enter into deliberations with our school choice colleagues about the shape of the legislation to be introduced or the initiative to be put before the people, we owe it to the children of this nation to rise above any petty jealousies or rivalries. We must truly listen to one another and treat each other with respect, and we must be willing to make the accommodations we know are needed to forge a winning team.

Chapter 32

Use U.S. Education Vouchers to Give Poor Families a Choice

John E. Coons and Stephen D. Sugarman

The following essay was first published as a guest editorial in the *Orange County Register,* the *Sacramento Bee,* and several other California daily newspapers in August of 1995.

A FEDERAL BUNDLE of about $6 billion annually goes, with many strings attached, to aid the education of disadvantaged children living in school districts of concentrated poverty. The Republican leadership in Congress is proposing to whittle this bundle down and then ship it to the states in relatively unrestricted block grants.

But Democrats such as ourselves are puzzled at this application of the "devolution" principle. The money should indeed devolve, but why send it to Sacramento, Albany, and other state capitals? The proper terminus for this largesse is the consumer whose good it is ultimately intended to serve. So why not give low-income families their own block grants in the form of federal schol-

arships that they could use in any school, public or private?

The policy arguments for this solution are straightforward. The hope of both the school and the family in the inner city rests upon making parents responsible for their own actions—beginning with the crucial responsibility of choosing their children's school. Of all the injuries that government has visited upon the low-income family, none is so gross and so unnecessary as the denial of school choice.

Up until age five, a child experiences the parent (even the inadequate parent) as advocate and champion. When it comes time for kindergarten, the child discovers the same parent to be helpless to alter whatever the school district decrees. The parents in turn learn to despise their own incapacity to nourish the minds and spirits of their children.

The experience in Milwaukee's small, publicly funded school choice plan indicates that, when given a chance, it is the exasperated welfare mother who transfers her child from the local public school to a participating private school. As a result, she is far more satisfied with the education her child receives.

It is one thing to criticize parental irresponsibility; it is another to impose it upon those who cannot buy their way out. The social price of the present system is apathy, ignorance, and hostility. The victims are fully aware that society allows wealthier parents to choose their

Federal scholarships for the children of the poor would be the functional equivalent of Pell grants, the current federal scholarship program at the college level. The individual grants to qualifying families should be large enough to induce new school providers to enter the urban market.

As a trial, we propose that eligible children who select private and religious schools would be entitled each year to receive a grant amounting either to the school's regular tuition or $5,000, whichever is less. The limits could be adjusted up or down to reflect the differences in costs for high school and elementary school.

> The hope of both the school and the family in the inner city rests upon making parents responsible for their own actions.... Of all the injuries that government has visited upon the low-income family, none is so gross and so unnecessary as the denial of school choice.

child's school by paying private tuition or by moving to fancy suburbs.

AS A policy to improve our urban schools, the market promises what "federal aid" cannot: competition that would reward the successful schools and close the failures. Evidence from several privately funded school voucher plans in San Antonio and Indianapolis confirms the belief that authentic choice improves educational outcomes for children of the poor. But in most cities today, even though most private schools cost significantly less to run than public schools, even a modest tuition still makes them financially inaccessible to the working class and the poor.

If a child chose an out-of-district public school, perhaps $2,000 beyond the regular school-spending amount would be transferred to the new school from the home district. Those who chose to remain in local public schools could qualify for $2,000 a year to be used on out-of-school enrichment programs selected by their families—such as individual tutoring or music lessons. Public school employees might well turn out to be major competitors in this new market for after-school, evening, and weekend offerings.

USING $5 billion or $6 billion this way could provide enormous freedom for several million poor children. It might even begin to make the hinges squeak on the rusted and rotten detention camps that far too many urban public schools have become.

Some advocates of devolution may agree with this approach and yet would prefer to let the states on their own decide whether to turn the federal money into vouchers for the poor. Unfortunately, there is little in American experience to justify such an expectation; the states have almost never used their own money to enlarge the autonomy of families in the realm of elementary and secondary schooling.

Moreover, many states face a peculiar legal problem. Although the U.S. Constitution appears congenial to the plan we have proposed, state constitutions may well forbid it. Perhaps three-quarters of all America's poor live in states, such as California, which forbid the expenditure of state funds for religious (and, in some states, all private) education. Even if state leaders were willing to convert block grants to scholarships, they would face litigation over using federal funds in this way. Such a legal tangle could be avoided, however, by direct federal subvention to the family.

HERE IS a venture for classical Republicans that has so far escaped their roster of market-oriented policies. Maybe such a plan could even win the support of Democrats in Congress who have expressed both their faith in the market and their concern for the poor.

Postscript by Bonsteel and Bonilla: In August of 1996, presidential candidate Robert Dole announced that he favored decreasing the size of the U.S. Department of Education bureaucracy and using the money saved for educational scholarships for deserving children. After Dole restated his support for school choice during the presidential debates, his opponent, President Clinton, replied, "I support school choice. If a local school district in Cleveland, or anyplace else, wants to have a private school choice plan, like Milwaukee did, let them have at it."

Chapter 33

The Next Round

Alan Bonsteel

Make no small plans, for they fail to stir men's blood.

— HENRY DAVID THOREAU

The balloting for California's Proposition 174 took place on the first Tuesday of November 1993. By that evening, we knew we'd gone down worse than expected. The next morning, I started calling people to a meeting I'd arranged for the following Friday. Although I tried not to let my voice betray my anxiety, I was wondering if anyone would actually show up. Were people too exhausted by the nonstop campaigning to continue? Too discouraged by the lopsided election result? Would people actually take a business day off to show up to pursue a dream?

I needn't have worried. On short notice, *forty-three* people showed up at the Dunfey Hotel in San Mateo. Nor were these ordinary people; they were highly accomplished, extremely intelligent people at the top of their careers who had gotten to where they were through energy and drive.

There was plenty to be disappointed about. The campaign had been disorganized and underfunded. The infighting had discouraged almost everyone. All agreed that the initiative draft had been problematic—although almost everyone had a different interpretation of just what the problems were. Yet the dedicated, optimistic people of what came to be known as the Dunfey Group could see only the positive. We'd gotten the issue of educational choice before the California people. The exit polls had shown that California voters now supported educational choice in principle by a 74 percent plurality. And the public education establishment had been exposed for what it is: a self-serving monopoly, bereft of ideas and devoid of idealism, with its schools shunned even by the people running them.

We now faced a difficult challenge in trying to qualify for the 1994 ballot. Because the November 1993 ballot had been a special election, called by Governor Pete Wilson because of an urgent need to pass a tax measure, the next ballot was only one year away. Few people have any idea of the advance planning that goes into a citizens' ballot initiative. To meet all the procedural deadlines required in order to qualify the measure at least 131 days before the next election, as specified in the California Constitution, proponents must file it with the attorney general's office *fourteen months* before the election, or lose precious signature-gathering days.

Those of us who compose the "Sugarmoe" group (John Coons, Stephen Sugarman, Terry Moe, Alan Bonsteel, Carlos Bonilla, and, as time permitted, Cliff Cobb) prepared our initiative draft in deep secrecy during the weekend before the election, applying the finishing touches on election day itself. Ernie Scherer, a real estate developer and former San Ramon public school board member, had written his own Community-Based Public Schools initiative that concentrated on choice within the public sector. Tipped off by me about the deadline crunch we were all facing, he had also prepared his draft before the election. On the morning after the election, a very sleepy Carlos Bonilla and I drove to Sacramento to file with the attorney general, with Scherer about an hour behind us. These two initiatives would have had only three months of signature-gathering time, instead of the usual five months, had they received the necessary backing. But that was not to be.

In time, four other initiatives were drafted: one by David Schumann and Kathleen O'Connell-Sundaram, who, with a number of other activists, formed the nucleus of the BayCARE group, headed by Rabbi Pinchas Lipner; one by the Phoenix Group, headed by the Los Angeles duo of financial planner David Barulich and attorney Bruce Adelstein; one by Berkeley commercial banker Carl Brodt; and one by Carl Brodt and Piedmont nuclear physicist David Anderson.

The Dunfey Group met monthly for almost two years, alternating meetings between San Mateo and the Los Angeles airport. John Walton was represented by San Diego businessman Rod Tompkins; Howard and Roberta Ahmanson were represented by Victor and Lois Porlier. The Catholic bishops were represented first by California Catholic Conference director Dr. Joseph McElligott, and then, on his retirement, by his successor, Robert Teegarden. Most of the key Dunfey people have been mentioned elsewhere in this book; a few who haven't include retired Bishop Mark Hurley, formerly of the Santa Rosa diocese; education consultant Dr. Robert Ferguson; attorney Brian Bennett, principal of the Blessed Sacrament School in San Diego; and Michael Masterson, one of the leaders of the Santa Clara Valley "Yes on 174" team. The Dunfey Group was chaired first by long-time political consultant Lorelei Kinder, who had held key posts in the Reagan administration, and later by Charles Heatherly, vice president of the Claremont Institute.

The goal of qualifying for the 1994 ballot proved to be elusive; in the time available, it was not possible to raise the necessary money. Focus then shifted to the 1996 ballot, with much of the leadership of the educational choice movement shifting to John Walton, of Wal-Mart stores. Walton had been a late donor to Prop. 174, but he took more and more interest in school choice as time passed. In his role as a business leader, he had become increasingly aware of the declining educational standards of new job applicants. A family man himself (and a former Stearman biplane crop-duster pilot), he is a good listener and a careful planner.

Together with San Francisco investor Bill Oberndorf, Walton formed the School Futures Research Foundation in San Diego, under the direction of the highly regarded Eugene Ruffin, a former executive with both IBM and Xerox. The extremely likable Jim Blew of Valencia—originally of the political consulting firm Winner/Wagner & Mandabach, where he put together an enviable success record working exclusively on initiatives, and now with Barchas, Anttila & Blew—was engaged to handle the political strategy, assisted in the initiative drafting efforts by ace law firm Nielsen, Merksamer, Parrinello, Mueller & Naylor of Mill Valley.

The School Futures group devoted extraordinary resources to opinion polls and focus groups on how to craft a winning school choice initiative. The results of these polls and others already available to us were mixed: although voters favor school choice in principle and are deeply dissatisfied with the public schools, they are also emotionally attached to public schools and suspicious of change. It appears possible to draft a school choice initiative that would start with a lead of more than 60 percent; when pitted against the kinds of deceptive arguments the opposition could be counted on to spend tens of millions of dollars to promote, however, it might well lose. It is, after all, far easier to defeat an initiative than to pass one; the former requires only that one plant doubt and confusion in the voters' minds.

The School Futures group ultimately decided to postpone its initiative efforts until 1998, meanwhile using its resources to educate voters, promote the concept of school choice, and concentrate on helping to establish new charter schools. They also decided to work in the legislative arena with a political action committee advised by a diverse group that includes the Reverend Lou Sheldon of the Traditional Values Coalition and Alice Huffman, former head of government affairs for the CTA. Huffman wrote in the July 1996 issue of the *California Journal* of her disillusionment with a public school establishment that is not addressing the collapse of our public schools.

The decision to postpone the initiative effort until 1998 was announced in August 1995. The School Futures group had become such an important player in the school choice movement in California that it was difficult to imagine an initiative effort without them. Most of the Dunfey Group members agreed to continue with a 1998 effort, the exception being the BayCARE group; it attempted to qualify for the 1996 ballot with an almost entirely volunteer signature drive, but fell short of the goal. The BayCARE effort at least kept the issue alive and before the voters and the news media. Although the initiative was an uncompromising measure that did not bring about a consensus among educational choice advocates, it did propose an innovative method of financing vouchers for current private school students, such that these vouchers would be funded *only* to the extent that money became available as students left more expensive public schools for less expensive private schools.

The state legislative analyst agreed that this method of financing would not require higher taxes—a critical element in any educational choice initiative. On the downside, however, this approach requires an extraordinarily long phase-in period of about twenty years to become fully operational, and it is impossible to specify in advance the size of the voucher for current private school students during that time period—information that, not surprisingly, both the voters and the private schools would like to know before making a decision.

The Dunfey Group has not met since August 1995 and is probably moribund, but the interchanges among the various players in this group helped to unite the movement and get it organized for a future effort. In the meantime, potential new support for educational choice has emerged from some exciting new directions. The January 18, 1996 issue of the *Wall Street Journal* carried an interview with Steven Jobs, cofounder of Apple Computer (to which he returned in December 1996 after several years' absence). Jobs reflected on how, as the young boss of Apple, he had imagined that technology would have a revolutionary impact on education. Now, he says, he has realized that "What's wrong with education can't be fixed with technology. . . . The problem is bureaucracy. I'm one of those people who believe the best thing we could ever do is go to a full voucher system. . . . God, how exciting that could be!" And it's exciting, of course, to think that one of the true pioneers of the Information Age might take on a leadership role in the crusade for school choice.

Almost everyone involved in the Prop. 174 effort is still active in the educational choice arena, one way or another. Kevin Teasley, the campaign's first executive director and later the director of fundraising, went on to become one of the cofounders of The Education Project, which publishes *The Report Card,* a hard-hitting investigative report about how badly our public schools are doing, coupled with news on developments in the world of educational choice. More recently, he moved to Indianapolis to become president of the American Education Reform Foundation.

Wilbert Smith, our champion speaker for Prop. 174, a former Pasadena school board member, and the holder of a Ph.D. in business administration, ran for the nonpartisan office of state superintendent of public instruction in

Wilbert Smith, Ph.D., school choice leader, public speaker extraordinaire, and one of the many living links between Proposition 174 and the next round in California's battle for educational freedom.

the June 1994 primary. In a crowded field, after a late start, and with an underfinanced campaign, he came in a close third behind Delaine Eastin and Maureen DeMarco, unfortunately missing the November runoff by a whisker. It's hard not to daydream a little about the witty, dynamic Smith debating the union operative Eastin in the runoff—a debate about the future of our schools that unfortunately never came to pass.

In July 1995, David Barulich announced the concept of *educational performance grants,* a new idea that was designed to help voucher advocates resolve the dilemma of ensuring accountability for the use of public funds while shielding private schools from excessive regulation. Although regulations ensuring accountability are necessary for garnering electoral support, minimizing their scope is necessary to effect any meaningful educational reform. To avoid this devil's bargain, Barulich proposed that children who do not attend public schools should receive public funds only *after* receiving passing scores on the same battery of examinations that public school students are required to pass before being promoted to the next grade. Requiring students to *earn* educational performance grants instead of giving them vouchers or tuition tax credits assures the electorate the level playing field, fiscal accountability, and protection from fraud that it demands, without the need for regulating private schools' hiring and enrollment policies, accreditation, curriculum, financial disclosures, facilities, etc. Barulich has proposed that students be allowed to take the tests once a year or, in cases of financial hardship, incrementally every two months. The latter schedule would allow low-income families who could not pay private school tuition fees up front to be able to participate in the program through state-funded loans at these two-month intervals.

Most states have constitutional amendments prohibiting aid to private schools—relics of religious intolerance and anti-Catholic agitation from the last half of the nineteenth century. Since vouchers are aid to families rather than to private schools, school choice programs passed by the legislatures in these states should be able to win the approval of objective state supreme courts that give the plans a fair hearing. In those states in which the state supreme court disagrees with this interpretation, however, educational performance grants would provide an additional measure of protection from conflict with state constitutions containing these restrictive amendments. This is because the grants could be used not just for private schools, but also for home schooling expenses or tutoring, and because no private school would ever cash a check issued by the state. The grants could thus provide a route to educational choice via the legislatures without their having to amend the state constitutions, or via the initiative statutory amendment process in states in which the constitution cannot be amended by initiative.

The major drawback of using testing as a qualification for the grants is the danger that the tests could, in effect, dictate the curricula offered by private schools. Imposing tests on an innovative, Sudbury Valley-style school, which allows children to learn at their own pace, would threaten the school's founding philosophy. Even Waldorf schools, first started eight decades ago, could be put at a competitive disadvantage, because they teach reading at a later age than most other schools. In practice, the burden of these tests would depend on the minimum passing scores set for the public school students by the elected state superintendent of public instruction. Most believe that the passing scores would be set low enough that the graduation rates from public schools would remain similar to today's: about 99 percent of those who hang in until the end of the twelfth grade. This should be no problem for students attending private schools. Barulich has also considered allowing alternative examinations (such as the Iowa Test and the Stanford Achievement Test) to be used as substitutes for the state's tests, to further thwart the potential for curricular hegemony.

Another drawback is that children from wealthier households could pass these exams more easily than the poorer children we really intend to help—at least until the latter had been exposed, for a year or two, to good schools, such as any of those profiled in Part II of this book. Barulich has considered this problem and has proposed implementing the grants initially as a ten-year pilot program in some of California's poorest school districts. Means testing of the grant amounts could also be applied.

Another *advantage* of the grants is that children in nontraditional educational programs that are excluded from most voucher plans (e.g., tutoring, home schooling, internships, apprenticeships, and enrollment in schools located overseas) could receive educational performance grants. These grants are an innovation that could help school choice advocates overcome some of the political and practical hurdles that have hampered further progress. The idea deserves broad dissemination and debate.[1]

A related subject is the concept of a national or statewide core curriculum, advocated most notably by the educator E. D. Hirsch, the author of *Cultural Literacy.* In his more recent book, *The Schools We Need and Why We Don't Have Them,* he developed a reasoned and well-supported argument for such a core curriculum, a cause championed most strongly in our group by Alan Wadsworth of Diablo, president of The Western Companies. Hirsch points to France as a country that has maintained high scholastic achievement despite far lower per student expenditures than in the United States (see Table 5.1). France requires that national standardized tests be administered to all elementary and secondary school students, 70 percent of whom are enrolled in government-operated schools, with the remaining 30 percent in private schools of choice operating with government subsidies. Although Hirsch does not make the following points, it is illuminating to note also that France has far lower dropout rates than the United States and that school violence is almost nonexistent, despite an influx of non-French-speaking immigrants from underdeveloped countries

---

[1] More information on this subject can be accessed by e-mail at barulich@earthlink.net. Or write to David Barulich, 1041 Rutland Ave., Los Angeles, CA 90042.

that is proportionally far larger than that which the United States has experienced.

It is difficult to argue with Hirsch's thesis that a core curriculum and nationwide testing have played a key role in the success of France's superb public school system. The authors of this book would argue as well, of course, that competition provided by the private schools of choice educating the other 30 percent of France's students has played at least as important a role.

Hirsch documents many other success stories, both overseas and in the United States, of well-developed core-curriculum programs. By contrast, it is hard not to be alarmed by the total lack of testing in California since the California Learning Assessment System (CLAS) was sunk, amid a storm of controversy, in 1994. It fell to a combination of criticism by education reformers who held that it was both simplistic and politically biased, and fierce lobbying by the public education establishment, which was determined to scuttle a test that made all too obvious the failure of our public schools.[2] It is a scandal, as well, that *more than half* of California State University freshmen arrive unprepared for college and are required to take remedial English (popularly known as "bonehead" English).

The concept of a core curriculum of English, science, mathematics, and history, enforced by statewide testing, could easily be compatible with a school choice program in principle. The risk, however, would be the same as with the testing in David Barulich's educational performance grants: the testing could dictate the curriculum and stifle innovation and freedom of choice. In fact, France and other countries, such as Japan, that are known for their core curricula are *not* known for educational innovation. On the other hand, examinations that public school students would be required to take along with private school students would have to be made lax enough to accommodate the lower standards in some government-operated schools, so that even innovative, nontraditional private schools would be expected to have no problem meeting their standards. Such statewide testing might also reassure the voters

---

[2]The history of the CLAS test and the decline in basic skills among California's public school students are detailed by Ben Boychuk in Briefing 1996–49, March 15, 1996, by the Claremont Institute, which has performed an enormous service to the citizens of California with its hard-hitting series of reports on education.

that private schools participating in a taxpayer-funded school choice program would not stray too far from the basics.

Perhaps a reasonable compromise might be universal testing, with full disclosure, that was not binding on grade-promotion decisions. Under such a compromise, schools would be required to disclose their average test performances publicly—and individual test results confidentially to parents—but they would be free to base their promotion decisions on their own published standards. Thus, parents would be free to choose a school that performed poorly on standardized tests, as long as they felt it offered other qualities they perceived to be of value.

In late 1995, Ernie Scherer did the groundwork for an initiative for the 1996 ballot that would have reformed existing public schools in some fundamental ways, most importantly by abolishing tenure for public school teachers. It would also have helped educational choice by prohibiting teachers unions from spending compulsory union dues for political purposes and by requiring that all political donations be voluntary. Scherer was assisted in this effort by Dr. Glenn Davis, the former associate state superintendent of public instruction under Wilson Riles, as well as political consultant Bob Hudak, businessman Archer Frey, and myself. We managed to raise about half the money needed to qualify an initiative that could go the statutory route rather than be a constitutional amendment, thereby requiring far fewer signatures for qualification.

Unfortunately, the CTA-affiliated United Teachers–Los Angeles (UTLA) countered our effort effectively by preparing a phony school reform initiative that would appear on the same ballot. Our research showed that, when faced with two similar initiatives, the voters would have voted for one or the other, but not both, thereby defeating both. (If two initiatives on the same subject *do* pass in the same election, then, under California law, the one that wins more votes takes full effect, and the other is invalidated.) Because of the high risk of burning out our grassroots workers and discouraging our donors on an effort that seemed to have little chance of success, our group postponed its work. The UTLA then withdrew its initiative, making it all the more obvious that its sole reason for existence had been to *thwart* school reform. Ultimately, neither initiative appeared on the 1996 ballot.

The UTLA has now taken these obstructionist tactics to their logical extreme by already having qualified, almost two years in advance, a new phony school reform initiative—commonly called "95/5"—for the June 1998 ballot. Its sole purpose appears to be to discourage school choice advocates from placing a *real* reform initiative on that ballot (see sidebar).

The 95/5 Hoax

The first round in the 1998 battle for school reform has already been fired, in the form of an "Educational Efficiency" initiative written by the United Teachers–Los Angeles. Dubbed "95/5" because of the percentages of tax funds that it *purports* to mandate for classroom spending as opposed to administration and overhead, the initiative was qualified as quietly as possible and was certified for the June 1998 ballot by the California secretary of state in August 1996.

This seemingly innocuous measure is a hoax. It defines administration and overhead so narrowly that the *current* cost of these items works out to only 6 percent of public school spending—only a tiny fraction of what is actually being spent. Thus, even if the 95/5 initiative achieved what it purports to—decreasing administrative and overhead costs from an alleged 6 percent to a new, improved 5 percent—direct classroom spending would increase by only 1 percent!

The only administration and overhead covered *at all* under 95/5 is at the school district level; it leaves untouched the bloated administration at the federal, state, county, and school-site levels. The initiative narrowly limits the definition of administration to a tiny handful of bureaucrats and specifically exempts *all* school-site personnel, so that actual reductions in the bureaucracy can be avoided entirely, simply by shuffling administrators to the schools, or even to the county or state levels of the system.

Even the definition of classroom spending is so vague as to be meaningless; the initiative text states that "'Direct services to pupils' means professional services rendered directly to pupils by certificated or licensed personnel, including, but not limited to, teachers, *supervisory personnel . . . and other support services personnel. . . .*" (Italics added.) Further, the narrow definitions of the tiny number of administrators included under the initiative are included as references to California Department of Education forms, which, of course, hardly anyone but the bureaucrats themselves will read. "District administration," for example, is defined as "reported in column 3 of Form J380 n(EDP Nos. 401 and 400) as that form existed on June 30, 1994 *or any equivalent successor to this reporting category or any subsequent form(s) which report the same class of expenditures.*" (Italics added.) Thus, even these flaky definitions are not codified into law, but *are simply referenced as bureaucratic forms that can be changed at will by the bureaucrats themselves!*

On February 9, 1990, the newsletter of the United Teachers–Los Angeles carried a scathing report by the president of the union claiming that, for the fiscal year 1988–89, $1.03 *billion,* or 31 percent of all Los Angeles Unified School District expenditures, went to the central and regional administrative offices *alone.* (See sidebar, "Numbers Don't Lie; Fat Cats Do," in Chapter 10.) This very same teachers union is now the proponent of an initiative claiming that district administration and overhead constitute only 6 percent of expenditures! Furthermore, as mentioned in Chapter 3, California's charter schools must kick back about 20 percent of their Average Daily Attendance (ADA) funding to their sponsoring district for "administration," even though the majority of them receive little or nothing in administrative support for it. Some even receive outright hostility from their "sponsoring" district because of the competition they provide and because of jealousy over the superior performance of charter schools at far less cost to the taxpayers. How is it that a system that demands a 20 percent kickback from the charter schools for district administrative "services" they never receive is spending only 6 percent on that district administration?

The 95/5 initiative is so toothless that even the powerful Association of California School Administrators probably won't bother opposing it. *The primary motivation of the 95/5 scam is not to promote school reform, but to thwart it, by giving voters the illusion that something is being done.* And for the November 1998 election, the California Teachers Association has prepared its "Penny for the Kids" measure to increase California's sales tax by one cent, all of which would go for increased teachers' salaries (perhaps the measure should be called "Penny for the Teachers"). They had already prepared this measure for the 1996 ballot and then shelved it because they thought they would have to fight another school choice initiative that year.

Perhaps the most odious consequence of the cynical 95/5 ploy is who gets hurt if the bureaucrats don't perform. If the school administrators or the school boards balk at even the minuscule administrative cutbacks mandated by 95/5, the penalty is *not* a cutback in the administrators' salaries, but rather a cutback in ADA funding, which would directly harm the students. Thus, the innocent victims of 95/5 would be the same ones who have always been those most hurt by a government monopoly on public education—our children.

Meanwhile, Michael Rothschild's Bionomics Institute in San Rafael has reemerged as a center for an educational choice initiative, in collaboration with Mike Ford, who moved to Texas in 1992 to become the president of Vindicator Corporation in Austin. Rothschild and Ford, who were among the original authors of Proposition 174, are highly respected by all in the educational choice movement, and they could well prove to be the intermediaries and peacemakers who put together a coalition for a 1998 initiative. In 1996, the Bionomics Institute engaged a summer intern, Avery Sheffield, to work on the school choice issue; among other accomplishments, she developed a Web site for school choice at **www.GetRealEd.org**.

In his State of the State address on January 5, 1996, California's Governor Wilson proposed his Opportunity Scholarships for children in schools scoring in the bottom 5 percent of achievement levels—a proposal that was communicated to the public by his press secretary, Sean Walsh, formerly Prop. 174's director of communications. Wilson is a shrewd and resourceful leader with a sharp ability to read the pulse of the voting public. With the strong support of then-speaker of the assembly, Curt Pringle (who is now the Republican Assembly leader), his Opportunity Scholarships bill passed the California Assembly in June 1996—but it did not pass the Senate.

Wilson's Opportunity Scholarships legislation was a brilliant yet simple proposal similar to one put forth by a long-time friend of educational choice,

Jerry Hume, until recently a member of California's state board of education. It is a relatively small, experimental proposal that allows the voting public the comfort of avoiding a wholesale change in our educational system. Since the participating children get only the state Average Daily Attendance money, and not the local and federal spending on education, the per student public school spending actually *increases*. Perhaps best of all, it is difficult to counter: how is the CTA going to rationalize forcing the very children it has most failed and abandoned to remain in the worst public schools?

There is much to be said for the educational choice movement's rallying behind a 1998 initiative for Wilson's proposal, run as a constitutional amendment. We would be championing an initiative that has already proved popular enough to pass the California Assembly and win crucial support among many key California newspapers that opposed Prop. 174. Although not all school choice advocates are enthusiastic about Wilson's Opportunity Scholarships, I know of no one in the movement who would oppose the program, which appears to make it unique among the proposals currently being debated.

Whatever we do, we *must* be united. The clock is ticking on 1998. We owe it to the schoolchildren of California and the nation to do our best to craft a consensus initiative, set aside our differences, and work together as a team to turn the tables on the CTA.

It is now clear that educational choice is inevitable, both in California and nationwide. All the other Western democracies have already adopted at least some form of educational choice that includes independent schools; we have yet to catch up. Ever more powerful supporters are coming forth to champion the cause of school choice. Demographic changes strongly favor choice: the older voters who, through rose-tinted glasses, look back at the public schools as they used to be are declining as a voting bloc and are being replaced by younger voters who know all too well how bad the public schools really are. Despite endless promises of reform, the schools continue to get worse and worse, and they are woefully unprepared for the tidal wave of new students inundating them.

Finally, and perhaps most importantly, we only need to win once. To maintain its monopoly, the public school establishment must win everywhere, every time. For us, a single victory in a single state will be the Holy Grail we are seeking: the statewide demonstration project that will prove once and for all the value of school choice and propel other state educational choice movements to victory after victory. While we in California hope we will be the first, it is a friendly competition, and we wish our colleagues in other states the best of luck.

Perhaps, just as the Berlin Wall came crashing down not so many years ago, the public education establishment will one day do the right thing and announce that holding children captive in a dysfunctional system no longer serves any purpose. On the other hand, maybe we'll need to be on the ballot several more times before ultimate victory. Either way, it is clear that, sooner or later, the American people will dismantle our government school monopoly and replace it with a system of educational freedom of choice.

Sooner, however, is much better than later.

Chapter 34

Free the Children

What drives educational choice advocates is the shining ideal of an educational system in which each child is an individual, each with needs that must be met and special gifts that deserve to be nurtured. We believe the working single mother who empties the wastebaskets at night should have the same right to direct the schooling of her child, the same right to *quality* education, that the bigshot in the penthouse office has always enjoyed.

Our dream is of a renaissance in education in which schools are true communities where every student has freely *chosen* to be there and *values* what that school has to offer. Our vision is of mature young adults who have a sense of meaning and purpose in their lives, who care about the well-being of others, who have the resourcefulness and creativity to adapt to a rapidly changing world, and who are fully engaged and playing the game of life for all it's worth.

As we approach the next millennium, what we need is nothing less than a paradigm shift in which the schools of the future teach in ways scarcely imagined now, and which challenge our youth to go far beyond everything that has gone before them. We want our children to explore the stars, to push the frontiers of cyberspace, and to solve the fundamental mysteries of cancer. We fervently hope that their generation will lead us into a better world in which hunger and need have been conquered, and in which we have finally set aside our weapons and learned to live together in peace.

We invite you to join us in our dream of an educational system that will take us into the twenty-first century, and that keeps alive the hopes and aspirations we have for our children.

Appendix

Organizations Supporting School Choice

In the last few years, there has been an explosive growth in the number of organizations supporting school choice. Most of them strongly favor a voucher system that would allow children to attend a private school—secular or religious—of their family's choice. We urge our readers to become actively involved in the school choice movement and to support the good work of these organizations in any way they can.

The following directory was compiled mainly from information kindly provided by the Alexis de Tocqueville Institution and the Blum Center for Parental Freedom in Education, to both of whom we are most grateful. Although the entire list from which this directory was taken—consisting of nearly 200 organizations—was too large to reprint in this book, a complete and continually updated version can be accessed on the Internet at www.GetRealEd.org. A hard copy can be obtained for a nominal fee by contacting Dr. Alan Bonsteel, 2291 Stockton Street, #407, San Francisco, CA 94133; telephone (415) 982-6403; fax (415) 982-6413.

The de Tocqueville Institution's list, "Inventory of Groups that Are Current and Potential Advocates for School Choice," compiled by Paul F. Steidler in 1996, contains extensive descriptions of 115 organizations and their activities. This list can be purchased from the Alexis de Tocqueville Institution, 1611 North Kent Street, Suite 901, Arlington, VA 22209; telephone (703) 351-4969.

David W. Kirkpatrick's book *School Choice: The Idea that Will Not Die* (Mesa, Arizona: Blue Bird Publishing, 1997), available from the publisher or in bookstores, also contains useful source information. Mr. Kirkpatrick is a Distinguished Fellow with the Blum Center for Parental Freedom in Education.

Local and Grassroots Organizations

Alliance of California Taxpayers and Involved Voters
P.O. Drawer 330
Aptos, CA 95001
(408) 688-8986
Contact: Jane Armstrong

Alliance for Children's Educational Excellence
7575 Shadow Lane
Sparks, NV 89434
(702) 786-4911
Contact: Leslie Porter

Bradley Foundation
777 East Wisconsin Ave., Suite 2345
Milwaukee, WI 53202
(414) 291-9915
Contact: Michael Joyce

Buckeye Institute for Public Policy Solutions
131 North Ludlow, Suite 317
Dayton, OH 45404
(937) 224-8352
Contact: Andrew Little

California Catholic Conference
1010 11th St., Suite 200
Sacramento, CA 95814
(916) 443-4851
Contact: Robert Teegarden

California Education Reform Alliance
P.O. Box 1459
Los Gatos, CA 95031
(408) 688-1926
Contact: Ed Burke

California Network of Educational Charters
751 Laurel St.
San Carlos, CA 94070
(415) 598-8192
Contact: Susan Steelman Bragato

California Taxpayers Association
921 11th St., Suite 800
Sacramento, CA 95814
(916) 441-0490
Contact: Larry McCarthy

Cascade Policy Institute
813 SW Alder, Suite 707
Portland, OR 97205
(503) 242-0900
Contact: Steve Buckstein

Charter Schools Project
CSU Institute for Education Reform
6000 J St.
Sacramento, CA 95819
(916) 278-4600
Contact: Eric Premack

Choice in Education Foundation
1821 University Ave. West, 305-S
St. Paul, MN 55104
(612) 484-1854
Contact: Mike Ricci

Citizens for Educational Freedom, California
6555 Tam O'Shanter Drive
San Jose, CA 95120
(408) 268-9614
Contact: Thomas Holford

Citizens for Educational Freedom, Indiana
837 Patterson Drive
South Bend, IN 46615
(219) 288-8726
Contact: Burnett Bauer

Citizens for Educational Freedom, Kansas
8530 Bradshaw
Lenexa, KS 66215
(913) 888-4455
Contact: John McDonough

Citizens for Educational Freedom, Kentucky
1904 Cliffview Lane
Florence, KY 41042
(606) 342-9029
Contact: Robert Hoffman

Citizens for Educational Freedom, Louisiana
P.O. Box 65196
Baton Rouge, LA 70896
(504) 344-7120
Contact: Kirby DuCote

Citizens for Educational Freedom, Massachusetts
P.O. Box 1109
East Orleans, MA 02643
(508) 255-5362
Contact: George Appell

Citizens for Educational Freedom, Michigan
511 Ballantyne
Grosse Pointe, MI 48236
(313) 831-1000
Contact: Marilyn Lundy

Citizens for Educational Freedom, Missouri
9333 Clayton Road
St. Louis, MO 63124
(314) 997-6361
Contact: Mae Duggan (founder of national CEF in 1959)

Citizens for Educational Freedom, Nevada
2005 Driscoll Drive
Reno, NV 89509
(702) 329-7870
Contact: David W. Hansen

Claremont Institute
1127 11th St., Suite 206
Sacramento, CA 95814
(916) 446-7924
Contact: Brian Kennedy

Coloradans for School Choice
5777 East Evans, Suite 101
Denver, CO 80222
(303) 692-9745
Contact: Ron Pierce

Delaware Public Policy Institute
1201 North Orange St.
Wilmington, DE 19899
(302) 655-7908
Contact: Joshua Pollak

Educational Excellence Coalition
4427 Thackeray Place, NE
Seattle, WA 98105
(206) 547-5916
Contact: Jim and Fawn Spady

Ethan Allen Institute
RR 1, Box 43
Concord, VT 05824
(802) 695-2555
Contact: John Mitchell

Evergreen Freedom Foundation
P.O. Box 552
Olympia, WA 98507
(360) 956-3482
Contact: Bob Williams

Friends of Choice in Urban Schools
2120 16th St., NW, Suite 100
Washington, DC 20009
(202) 387-4000
Contact: Malcolm Peabody

Georgia Parents for Better Education
1355 Peachtree St., NE, Suite 1150
Atlanta, GA 30309
(404) 876-3335
Contact: Glenn A. Delk

Goldwater Institute
201 North Central Ave.
Phoenix, AZ 85004
(602) 256-7018
Contact: Jeffrey Flake

Heartland Institute
800 East Northwest Highway, Suite 1080
Palatine, IL 60067
(847) 202-3060
Contact: Joseph Bast

Howard Jarvis Taxpayers Association
621 South Westmoreland Ave., Suite 202
Los Angeles, CA 90005
(213) 384-9656
Contact: Joel Fox

James Madison Institute
2017 Delta Blvd., Suite 102
Tallahassee, FL 32317
(904) 386-3131
Contact: Dr. J. Stanley Marshall

Jersey City, Office of the Mayor
City Hall
Jersey City, NJ 07302
(201) 547-5200
Contact: Mayor Bret Schundler

John Locke Foundation
1304 Hillsborough St.
Raleigh, NC 27605
(919) 828-3876
Contact: John Hood

John N. Olin Foundation
330 Madison Ave., 22nd Floor
New York, NY 10017
(212) 661-2670
Contact: James Piereson

Maine School Choice Coalition
12 Belmont Road
Brunswick, ME 04011
(207) 729-1590
Contact: Frank J. Heller

Manhattan Institute
Center for Educational Innovation
52 Vanderbilt Ave.
New York, NY 10017
(212) 599-7000
Contact: Lawrence Mone

Nevada Policy Research Institute
P.O. Box 20312
Reno, NV 89515
(800) 786-9602 or (702) 786-9600
Contact: Judy Cresanta

Oregon Public Charter Schools Committee
3957 East Burnside
Portland, OR 97214
(503) 234-4600
Contact: Dr. Richard Meinhard

Oregon School Choice Task Force
1630 Hillwood Court, S
Salem, OR 97302
(503) 363-0899
Contact: Dr. Lowell Smith

Pacific Research Institute
755 Sansome St., Suite 450
San Francisco, CA 94111
(415) 989-0833
Contact: Lance Izumi

Parental Advocates of Choice in Education
467 Bloomfield Ave.
Bloomfield, CT 06022
(203) 242-4362
Contact: Matthew Boyle

Parents & Taxpayers for School Choice
4210 36th Ave., NE
Olympia, WA 98516
(360) 456-8343
Contact: Ron Taber

Partners Advancing Values in Education
1434 West State St.
Milwaukee, WI 53233
(414) 342-1505
Contact: Daniel McKinley

Paul Gann's Citizens Committee
9745-D Business Park Drive
Sacramento, CA 95827
(916) 366-3500
Contact: Richard Gann

Public Interest Institute
600 North Jackson St.
Mt. Pleasant, IA 52641
(319) 385-3462
Contact: Dale Bails

REACH Alliance
600 North Second St., Suite 400
Harrisburg, PA 17108
(717) 238-1878
Contact: Christopher Friend

School Choice Advocates
35 Merwyn Ave.
Rochester, NY 14609
(716) 546-1400
Contact: Howard Budd

South Carolina Policy Council Education Foundation
1419 Pendleton St.
Columbia, SC 29201
(803) 779-5022
Contact: Edward T. McMullen, Jr.

Texas Public Policy Foundation
P.O. Box 40519
San Antonio, TX 78229
(210) 614-0080
Contact: Jeff Judson

Washington Institute for Policy Studies
P.O. Box 24645
Seattle, WA 98124
(800) 546-4460 or (206) 938-6300
Contact: Bill Baldwin

National Organizations

Alexis de Tocqueville Institution
1611 North Kent St., Suite 901
Arlington, VA 22209
(703) 351-4969
Contact: Paul Steidler

Alliance for Catholic Education
University of Notre Dame
Notre Dame, IN 46556
(219) 631-7052
Contact: Mike Novak

American Education Reform Foundation
3802 Springfield Overlook
Indianapolis, IN 46234
(317) 328-4711
Contact: Kevin Teasley

American Enterprise Institute for Public Policy Research
1150 17th St., NW
Washington, DC 20036
(202) 862-5919
Contact: Dr. John Fonte

American Legislative Exchange Council
910 17th St., NW, 5th Floor
Washington, DC 20006
(202) 466-3800
Contact: Duane Parde

Americans for Tax Reform
1320 18th St., NW, Suite 200
Washington, DC 20036
(202) 785-0266
Contact: Jim Lucier

Association of American Educators
26012 Marguerite Parkway, Suite 333
Mission Viejo, CA 92692
(800) 704-7799 or (714) 582-3206
Contact: Gary Beckner

Association of Christian Schools International
P.O. Box 35097
Colorado Springs, CO 80935
(719) 528-6906
Contact: Ken Smitherman

Ball, Skelly, Murren & Connell, Attorneys
511 North 2nd St.
Harrisburg, PA 17108
(717) 232-8731
Contact: William Ball

Bionomics Institute
2173 East Francisco Blvd., Suite C
San Rafael, CA 94901
(415) 454-1000
Contact: Michael Rothschild

Black America's Political Action Committee
2029 P St., NW, Suite 302
Washington, DC 20036
(202) 785-9619
Contact: Alan Keyes

Blum Center for Parental Freedom in Education
Marquette University
Brooks Hall, Room 209
Milwaukee, WI 53201
(414) 288-7040
Contact: Dr. Quentin L. Quade

Bradley Project on the 90s
1150 17th St., NW, 10th Floor
Washington, DC 20036
(202) 862-7180
Contact: William Kristol

Cato Institute
1000 Massachusetts Ave., NW
Washington, DC 20001
(202) 842-0200
Contact: David Boaz

Center for Education Reform
1001 Connecticut Ave., NW, Suite 204
Washington, DC 20036
(800) 521-2118 or (202) 822-9000
Contact: Jeanne Allen

Center for Equal Opportunity
815 15th St., NW, Suite 928
Washington, DC 20005
(202) 639-0803
Contact: Linda Chavez

Center for New Black Leadership
815 15th St., NW, Suite 930-N
Washington, DC 20005
(202) 638-0651
Contact: Brian Jones

Center for Policy Studies
59 West 4th St.
St. Paul, MN 55102
(612) 224-9703
Contact: Dr. Ted Kolderie

Center for School Change
Hubert Humphrey Institute of Public Affairs
University of Minnesota
301 19th Ave. South
Minneapolis, MN 55455
(612) 625-3506
Contact: Joe Nathan

Center for the Study of Popular Culture
9911 West Pico Blvd., Suite 1290
Los Angeles, CA 90035
(310) 843-3699
Contact: David Horowitz

CEO America
P.O. Box 1543
Bentonville, AR 72712
(501) 273-6957
Contact: Fritz Steiger

Christian Educators Association International
P.O. Box 41300
Pasadena, CA 91114
(818) 798-1124
Contact: Forrest L. Turpen

Citizens for Educational Freedom
927 South Walter Reed Drive, Suite 1
Arlington, VA 22204
(703) 486-8311
Contact: Patrick J. Reilly

Clare Booth Luce Policy Institute
112 Elden St., Suite P
Herndon, VA 20170
(703) 318-0730
Contact: Michelle Easton

Committee for Public Autonomous Schools
2946 Macomb St., NW
Washington, DC 20008
(202) 363-8510
Contact: Dorothy Goodman

Commonwealth Foundation
3544 North Progress Ave., Suite 101
Harrisburg, PA 17110
(717) 671-1901
Contact: Don Eberly

Competitive Enterprise Institute
1001 Connecticut Ave., NW
Washington, DC 20036
(202) 331-1010
Contact: Marlo Lewis, Jr.

Congress of Racial Equality
30 Cooper Square
New York, NY 10003
(212) 598-4000
Contact: Roy Innis

Concerned Women for America
370 L'Enfant Promenade, SE, Suite 800
Washington, DC 20024
(202) 488-7000
Contact: Laurel A. MacLeod

Council for American Private Education
18016 Mateny Road, Suite 140
Germantown, MD 20874
(301) 916-8460
Contact: Joe McTighe

Council of 100
381 N St., SW
Washington, DC 20035
(202) 775-5496
Contact: Milton Bins

Doyle Associates
110 Summerfield Road
Chevy Chase, MD 20815
(301) 986-9350
Contact: Denis Doyle

Educational Freedom Foundation
927 South Walter Reed Drive, Suite 1
Arlington, VA 22204
(703) 486-8311
Contact: Patrick J. Reilly

Education Leaders Council
1001 Connecticut Ave., NW, Suite 204
Washington, DC 20036
(202) 822-9000
Contact: Gretchen Wolfe

Education Policy Institute
4401-A Connecticut Ave.
Washington, DC 20008
(202) 244-7535
Contact: Myron Lieberman

Empower America
1776 I St., NW, Suite 890
Washington, DC 20006
(202) 452-8200
Contact: Cherie Harder

Family Research Council
801 G St., NW
Washington, DC 20001
(202) 393-2100
Contact: Robert G. Morrison

Free Congress Foundation
717 Second St., NE
Washington, DC 20002
(202) 546-3000
Contact: Paul Weyrich

Griffith & Rogers, Attorneys
1101 Connecticut Ave., NW, Suite 800
Washington, DC 20036
(202) 333-4936
Contact: Lanny Griffith

Heritage Foundation
214 Massachusetts Ave., NE
Washington, DC 20002
(202) 546-4400
Contact: Thomas W. Wielgus

Hudson Institute
1015 18th St., NW, Suite 300
Washington, DC 20036
(202) 223-7770
Contact: Chester E. Finn, Jr.

Independent Institute
134 98th Ave.
Oakland, CA 94603
(510) 568-6047
Contact: David Theroux

Individual Rights Foundation
9911 West Pico Blvd., Suite 1290
Los Angeles, CA 90035
(310) 843-3699
Contact: David Horowitz

Institute for Contemporary Studies
720 Market St., 4th Floor
San Francisco, CA 94102
(415) 981-5353
Contact: Robert B. Hawkins, Jr.

Institute for Justice
1717 Pennsylvania Ave., NW, Suite 200
Washington, DC 20006
(202) 955-1300
Contact: William H. Mellor

Landmark Legal Foundation
457-B Carlisle Drive, 2nd Floor
Herndon, VA 20170
(703) 689-2370
Contact: Mark Levin

Milton and Rose D. Friedman Foundation
One American Square, Suite 2440
Indianapolis, IN 46282
(317) 681-0745
Contact: Gordon St. Angelo

National Association for the Legal Support of Alternative Schools
P.O. Box 2823
Santa Fe, NM 87501
(505) 471-6928
Contact: Ed Nagel

National Catholic Education Association
1077 30th St., NW, Suite 100
Washington, DC 20007
(202) 337-6232
Contact: Dr. Leonard DeFiore

National Parents Alliance, Inc.
100 Hart St., Suite 1B
Brooklyn, NY 11206
(718) 388-3765
Contact: William Andrews

National Tax Limitation Committee
151 North Sunrise Ave., Suite 901
Roseville, CA 95661
(916) 786-9400
Contact: Lew Uhler

National Taxpayers Union
713 Maryland Ave., NE
Washington, DC 20002
(202) 543-1300
Contact: David Keating

New Citizenship Project
1150 17th St., NW, 5th Floor
Washington, DC 20036
(202) 822-8333
Contact: John P. Walters

Of The People Foundation
2111 Wilson Blvd., Suite 700
Arlington, VA 22201
(703) 351-5051
Contact: Greg Erken

Reason Foundation
3415 South Sepulveda Blvd., Suite 400
Los Angeles, CA 90034
(310) 391-2245
Contact: Robert Poole

School Futures Research Foundation
2120 San Diego Avenue, Suite 200A
San Diego, CA 92110
(619) 459-2177
Contact: Eugene Ruffin

William J. Tobin & Associates
3612 Bent Branch Court
Falls Church, VA 22041
(703) 941-4329
Contact: William J. Tobin

Index

About the Authors

ALAN BONSTEEL was the campaign director for one of the earliest efforts to put educational choice before the voters of the United States: the Coons-Sugarman initiative of 1980-1981. He has studied systems of educational choice in twelve countries and is California's top expert on comparative educational choice overseas. He was the most widely published author during California's Proposition 174 battle for school choice, reaching 6 million readers through the editorial pages of California's newspapers, and—after Wilbert Smith—he was the campaign's second most active speaker. A physician in his professional life, he divides his time between family practice and emergency medicine. He lives in San Francisco.

CARLOS A. BONILLA is a molecular biologist and human geneticist who has published extensively in the fields of toxicology, pharmacology, and education. A former National Institutes of Health Special Research Fellow in cardiovascular disease, Dr. Bonilla has devoted much of his time during the past fifteen years—as a consultant, columnist, and author of six books—to the problems affecting K-12 students in general and Latino students in particular. He is California's foremost expert on state dropout rates, especially for Hispanic students, and he testified in 1991 before the Little Hoover Commission on the systematic underreporting of dropout rates by the State Department of Education. He lives in Stockton, California.

JOHN E. COONS is Professor Emeritus at the School of Law (Boalt Hall), University of California at Berkeley. Together with Stephen D. Sugarman, he was a proponent of the 1978 *Serrano* decision in the California Supreme Court, which brought equity to public school financing in California. From 1978 through 1981, Drs. Coons and Sugarman led the first serious political campaigns for school choice in the United States. Dr. Coons is the author, with Sugarman and William Clune, of *Private Wealth and Public Education* (1970). With Sugarman, he also wrote *Education by Choice: The Case for Family Control* (1978) and *Scholarships for Children* (1992).

MILTON FRIEDMAN wrote *Capitalism and Freedom* in 1962; it was the first book to advocate a voucher system for elementary and secondary education in the United States. In 1980, with his wife, Rose, he wrote *Free to Choose*, which continued their commentary on school choice, as did their television series of the same name. Dr. Friedman was active in the Prop. 174 campaign (1993), which would have introduced a universal voucher system in California. In 1996, he and his wife established the Milton and Rose D.

Friedman Foundation for Educational Choice, in Indianapolis, Indiana; its President and CEO is Gordon St. Angelo. Dr. Friedman is currently a Senior Research Fellow at the Hoover Institution on War, Revolution and Peace, at Stanford University. He was awarded the Nobel Prize in Economics in 1976.

JAMES HORSMAN has been a high school teacher in the Los Angeles Unified School District for the past thirteen years. He currently teaches basic mathematics in grades 9 through 12. He holds a B.A. in economics from California State University at Sacramento and has done several years of graduate work toward a Ph.D. in economics and mathematics at the University of Southern California. His e-mail address is jhorsman@jovanet.com.

STEPHEN D. SUGARMAN is the Agnes Roddy Robb Professor of Law and the Director of the Family Law Program of the Earl Warren Legal Institute at the University of California at Berkeley. Since 1970 he has contributed to the school choice movement by, among other things, designing school choice plans, drafting school choice statutes and initiatives, evaluating the possible legal challenges to such reforms, and participating in lawsuits on behalf of families seeking school choice as a legal remedy. Dr. Sugarman is the author, with John Coons and William Clune, of *Private Wealth and Public Education* (1970). With Coons, he also wrote *Education by Choice: The Case for Family Control* (1978) and *Scholarships for Children* (1992). He is also the coeditor of *All Our Families: New Policies for a New Century* (1997).

About ICS

Founded in 1974, the Institute for Contemporary Studies (ICS) is a non-profit, nonpartisan policy research institute. To fulfill its mission to promote self-governing and entrepreneurial ways of life, and to help spur policy reform, ICS sponsors a variety of programs and publications on a wide range of governance issues, including the key areas of education, entrepreneurship, the environment, leadership, and social policy.

Through its imprint, ICS Press, the Institute publishes serious, innovative, and readable books that will further the understanding of these issues among scholars, policy makers, and the wider community of citizens. The Press has published more than a hundred scholarly books—plus hundreds of booklets and newsletters—which include the writings of eight Nobel laureates, and which have been influential in setting the nation's policy agenda.

Other ICS Press books about educational choice and school reform include *Break These Chains* by Daniel McGroarty; *Character First: The Hyde School Difference* by Joseph W. Gauld; *What Are We Trying to Teach Them Anyway: A Father's Focus on School Reform* by Ronald K. Pierce; *Responsive Schools, Renewed Communities* by Clifford W. Cobb; and *Winning the Brain Race: A Bold Plan to Make Our Schools Competitive* by David T. Kearns and Denis P. Doyle.